THE MADONNA CODE

Love & Light
Always
♡
Kim Y

THE
MADONNA
CODE

MYSTERIES OF THE DIVINE
FEMININE UNVEILED

KAREN McGREGOR

First Published in Great Britain 2010 by Influence Publishing
(an imprint of Bookshaker)

© Copyright Karen McGregor

Cover photo and art work: Amber Light Photography
Editors: Sylvia Taylor and Esther Hart
Book Design: Joe Gregory

PRAISE

"In this time of uncertainty, *The Madonna Code* shows us how to transcend personal challenges and call forth Sacred Heart Wisdom. This book is a gem and will bring you back to your Highest Self."

James Twyman, Peace Troubadour and bestselling author of *The Moses Code* and *The Barn Dance*

"The Madonna Code provides a provocative and passionate look at the feminine face of God. Karen McGregor focuses on heart-opening processes and insights to bring you to the meeting point of your humanity and divinity."

Caroline Sutherland, bestselling author of *The Body Knows: How to Tune In to Your Body and Improve Your Health*

"Karen has a deep understanding of how to combine the spiritual with the practical. In *The Madonna Code* she provides us with a wonderful guide for how we can use the symbolic figure of Mary and find what we really want in life—love, joy, peace and connection with something bigger than us."

Jan Janzen, bestselling author, international speaker

"The sheer beauty of Karen McGregor's writing, together with her deep spiritual insight, propels the reader straight to the heart. In this place of purity, we find the Madonna. It's a journey through the shadows to the discovery of one's spiritual magnificence."

Rev. Carrie Hunter, Trans-denominational minister

"*The Madonna Code* takes you on an inner journey to discover the core of the feminine, guiding you to access this presence within. Your heart will open through Karen's personal stories and introspective exercises as you look deeply and embrace the feminine within you. Discover truthfully who you are and how you can authentically express the feminine and bring balance and healing to our world."

Kris Steinnes, founder of Women of Wisdom Foundation and bestselling author of the award-winning *Women of Wisdom: Empowering the Dreams and Spirit of Women*

"Reading *The Madonna Code* brought me Divine Joy and Love. Through Karen's own experiences and deep understanding of the Divine Feminine, she has captured the true essence of self-love and Universal Love from the All. This book is for both women and men to explore and understand their Divine Feminine within. A mastery of self exploration and openness to bring our consciousness to a new level of appreciation and love. Our angels are excited to have *The Madonna Code* shared worldwide."

Cindy Smith, creator of the Angel Empowerment Program (AEP™); Certified Angel Therapy Practitioner (ATP®)

"Karen invites us inside. She shares her unfolding and the locating of herself within the Divine Feminine. Her poignant and personal stories are reflections on one woman's awakening, yet they feel universal; many will relate. In her own words we are called "to live in the Divine and to be human" and as she points out, given this, we must learn to surrender and "to live in paradox". There is no black and white, either/or in spirituality, there is simply ALL THAT IS. Karen shares how she became comfortable with this paradox and invites you to do the same."

Jonina Kirton, poet/author and Sacred Circle facilitator

"A Must Read! *The Madonna Code* contains a key that can help men and women unlock pathways to unconditional love, passion and bliss. Karen's book is filled with profound wisdom and practical exercises that can transform individuals, communities and nations."

Andrew Rezmer, producer of ConsciousLivingRadio.org

"Karen McGregor digs deep into the 'Heart of the Queen' from her own soul with brilliant pearls of wisdom on Sacred Leadership. She speaks from her core with raw, honest, insights and personal observations that moved me to stand up to say, "You are a powerful woman!" *The Madonna Code* reveals the Divine Dance between our inner strengths of the masculine and loving care of the feminine, while encouraging us to step into being the powerful leaders we are meant to be. Woo-men around the world are ready for the message of *The Madonna Code*. Run, don't walk, to the bookstore and then share it with your friends. It will change your life!"

Nancy Kerner, creator of Vision Dancer Productions and author of soon-to-be- released, *You are A Powerful Woman!*

"*The Madonna Code* exemplifies the missing element of conscious oneness with God…the return to the Divine Feminine within humanity. With wisdom, grace and love, Karen shares her personal journey and powerful message. She eloquently guides us in our understanding of our quest into truth and return to the true essence of who we really are. Thank you for guiding my heart home."

Hannelore, M.S.C., M.S.H., author of soon-to-be-released, *Ignite Your 6th Sense: The Power of Your Intuition*

*To my mother, who brings
me home to my heart.*

CONTENTS

Acknowledgments

I AM ETERNALLY GRATEFUL to the many people who supported the creation of this book. My deepest appreciation to my inspirational book-writing coach and publisher, Julie Salisbury, who ceaselessly held my vision and my hand throughout the past few months. To my editor, Sylvia Taylor, for her keen insight and understanding of the depths of the human heart translated into words. Great thanks to Esther Hart for efficient line editing and gentle wisdom. My awe and gratitude for photographer and artist, Karen Learmonth of Amber Light Photography, who captured the Madonna's essence with her artistic genius and intuitive heart. Profound thanks to the Spiritual Authors Circle for encouraging and inspiring me to bring this message to people around the world, and especially to Kim Tebbutt, whose love of Mary and the angels lights up every room she enters. To the glorious Nancy Kerner, for being my role model; your love and Divine Feminine wisdom are embedded in every page of this book. And to my writing partner, Jonina Kirton, for her gentle encouragement and deep insights from the very beginning of the book's inception.

I have a circle of precious friends who have supported me with their love, patience and wisdom. They taught me the art of gentleness, and for that I am profoundly grateful.

From the depths of my heart, thank you Mary McTier, Rita Koivunen and Wendi McNally. My deepest appreciation to Sharon Delalla, Mary Ellen Sanajko and Christine Pollock who taught me perseverance, commitment and courage in the face of adversity. And to Andrew Rezmer, for your constant support and relentless commitment to this book and its message; I am eternally grateful.

I am blessed with two beautiful sons, Matthew and Mitchell. Their joyful and passionate energy brings the angels out to play. Thanks to my Earth Mother, Marita, for her patience and boundless commitment to helping me in the completion of this book. And to my Divine Mother ~ words cannot describe my immense gratitude. You have guided my heart and this book; your radiant love whispers eternal light into these pages.

ͺINTRODUCTION

MY DEEP SADNESS sits in the depth of my heart and my mind reaches in with a claw to implant guilt. I recognize this intruder, try to push him away, tell him that I just want to be alone in this loss.

Three years ago I knew I must leave my marriage. That is, my soul and deepest feminine heart knew that our relationship as a marriage was complete. Sitting quietly in my heart, this was intuitively clear. I felt peace in my body and a sense of courage. With this came tears shed in snow banks, grassy fields and corridors.

I heard my ego voice and the voices of concerned friends question my decision: "You have a husband that loves you, a happy home, two gorgeous children together, a mother who shares your home and loves and supports both of you. Why?"

I could not answer. My mind could not come up with reasons that would "justify" leaving, justify destroying our marriage, jeopardizing the children we nurtured together and our common bonds within our community. The best I could do was tell people that we grew apart; that we did not have an intimate connection. The pat answers, the soft excuses.

My soul was relentless in the completion of our relationship. How was I to relay that to people who had never felt or recognized their soul's compass; or at least, never been led to do something outrageously unreasonable? I could not and began to close my heart more and more to those who reached out to understand. My male self, protective and action oriented, made a decision to shroud my heart and not let anyone or anything in that might break what was so close to shattering.

I let the pieces of my life fall and surrendered to the great misery at my feet. Not only was I separating from my husband of fourteen years but I also lost both business partners and spent the summer in hospital with my son, who was healing from a broken leg.

What I didn't know was that breaking down, shattering the bits of my identity, was the only act that would bring me to my abandoned feminine heart. It was my introduction to the experience of the Divine Feminine.

It was here that I met Mary. Growing up Catholic, I had an idea of who Mary was based on scriptures and homilies, but I had never had the experience of Mary. I had never had the heart-based connection to her as Divine Feminine essence. My understanding was mind-based and had not touched the edges of my heart. The intellectual understanding of a historical figure gave me little motivation to get to know her. The same can be true of getting to know my own feminine divinity. It held little interest for me.

I had never known true desperation until that summer. In the not-knowing, in the mystery, I saw images of Mary in my mind and felt her warmth in my heart. I began to pray and discover what unconditional love feels like in my body. I continued to reach out to Mary, as woman and Goddess, because something deep within me wanted her help. Help to leave Earth, if only for a while, and be with her, wherever that was. I threw myself, arms and legs splayed, onto my bed, begging to be released from the nightmare I had created.

I must admit that I expected nothing to change. But on one particularly trying day, I heard Mary say, "Focus on your heart." As I did this, my heart warmed and was followed by an intense heat that within minutes felt like a burning fire. I felt weightless, as if I was part of the air around me, and a warm white light bathed me in love. I did nothing except be a part of this heaven; I did not think, act, or move. I simply was one with the All.

When I returned back on the gentle direction of Mary, I knew that I had experienced the very heart of the Sacred Feminine. The very thing I tried to stuff out of existence in an effort to protect myself was the saving grace of my life.

My journey into the heart of the Divine Feminine remains a journey. It is not an end point or an answer. A discovery throughout this journey has been the realization that the Code held by Mary, the Madonna, cannot be opened in the traditional sense—in the male-orientated way of finding the one word, one concept, one key to unraveling the mystery. This book encourages you to stop searching for what is missing and instead, look within to unveil the Code of your heart. It invites you to receive this Code by experiencing different aspects of your feminine God nature.

The chapters in this book all center on aspects or "hearts" of Mary that unveil your Divine Feminine essence. The heart of Mary is a symbol that has been revered and shown in sculptures and paintings around the world. Similar to the heart of Jesus, ripped wide open in raw form, Mary's heart is not veiled—there is a sense that she has broken through her human conditioning to enter the great mystery of radical, all encompassing love. While she has been associated with Catholicism, her love for humanity and all of Life is boundless and cannot be confined to religion; it cannot be grasped by ego and intellect, which want scientific proof and historical evidence. The experience of this love and this heart within is beyond the reasoning mind.

As I reflected on and felt the Mary Heart in my own body, I came to realize that it has within it all the aspects of the Divine Feminine that I have come to understand and experience. Some of these aspects, like the essence of the Mother Heart, can be viewed as literal, yet this book focuses mainly on the symbolic parts of Mary as woman and deity. For ease of reading and revisiting processes, I have organized these parts into four Hearts that are all part of the Divine Feminine: The Virgin Heart, the Mother Heart, the Heart of the Goddess and the Heart of the Queen.

The Virgin Heart enters the purity of the sacred feminine relationship to self, other and Source; a purity that can be found in the present moment where love exists without conditions, assumptions, beliefs and expectations. The Heart of the Mother (which we all have regardless of whether we have children or not) is a journey into the acceptance of both the light and shadow sides; it gives

4

practical processes to honor and accept ourselves fully. As we honor and accept self, we begin the mothering of all of Life, which is in desperate need of this most transformative energy. The Heart of the Goddess is the experience of the essential nature of your feminine power—your experience of self as Divine Love and you as a vessel through which Divine Guidance flows and guides, with a new confidence that mystifies and magnetizes; a confidence that is not forced or found on the outside, but lives eternally on the inside. The Heart of the Queen is leadership through unity; it invites a new paradigm where communities of women regularly gather in circle and return to the remembrance of who they are; a time where women welcome their Divine Masculine to harmonize with their Sacred Feminine. It is a vision for a new world where all of the Mary Hearts are felt through every woman, and every woman becomes a leader, guiding the way for others with love and compassion. The final chapter ends with a call to unveil our Divine Feminine and take our role as the leaders of a time in history where new consciousness is rapidly needed. I believe our world can enter this time without destroying itself if enough of us can shine our light consciously and actively, starting now, in the present moment.

My journey is to unveil the Mary within. To hear the woman Mary who lived a life of challenges that she met with radical love; to surrender to all that is, through the vast and radical love of the heart; to listen, receive and nurture; to love and release and love and release, as she did her entire life. To feel the gentleness of the human heart whisper truth as I turn this over to you, in the form of this book. When you open it, open to all within you as you would to the heart of your beloved; let your body feel the ecstasy of truth and the freedom of surrender as you experience the Hearts of Mary, the Hearts I discovered on my journey and the Hearts that have always been with you and are with you now.

THE EXPERIENCE OF THE CODE

In each chapter, there are several spiritual exercises and processes that will enrich your experience of the Code. You will find them highlighted as "Sacred Practice". I believe that without experience, the insights lack opportunity to be used in daily life. By engaging in the processes and individual exercises, your *knowing* of an insight will become the *living* of it. I believe in the power of spiritual discipline. The word "discipline" is often shunned in North America, and I had to inquire into my own discomfort around it.

When I reflect on self-discipline, I am aware of how much of my past conditioning and beliefs are connected to it. Growing up with German parents whose cultural values focused on hard work as the path to success, I adopted the belief that I was worthy if I over-achieved and defeated challenges to reach my destination. I embraced self-discipline my whole life to keep everyone in my family happy and to achieve the goal of balance. Nothing about discipline was a process for me. It was entirely a "doing" with an end result that was assessed and judged.

If I didn't succeed in getting what I wanted and the self-discipline "failed", I carried the burden of shame, not being good enough, and feeling that I needed somehow to be punished; that I no longer belonged to the tribe that *was* disciplined and *did* achieve. I felt that to be part of this tribe was to prove my specialness in the world and my confidence and certainty about my future.

But what if I no longer knew what I wanted? What if I was uncertain of the future in both my relationships and work? Could I be disciplined in a state of uncertainty? I was convinced that was impossible so I resisted any form of spiritual practice. This resistance turned into my conditioned inner voices saying that I would never be able to follow through on what really made my heart sing and that my intuition and deep connection to Spirit would never be a reality.

It took me a couple of years before I began to recognize how that related to true spiritual discipline. Spirituality is not run on the conditioned mind and the voices of my core beliefs; it is not the goal, the trophy, or the award. It is something that I do out of love to know myself, others and God in the most intimate relationship possible. It is a process that does not make anyone more special or gifted than the next; rather, true spiritual discipline results in the dissolving of specialness and separateness, moving always towards union and radical love. It is a Divine Feminine principle.

One block you may encounter on your spiritual path is your will to control that which you call God. This is perhaps the biggest form of resistance to continuing spiritual discipline. I realized that once I experienced radical love and had glimpses of divine truths, my ego mind wanted to direct this path more than ever before. It was relentless in devising ways to keep me safe and protected from the unreasonable and unpredictable life of Spirit.

It is also important to be aware of your relationship to the many words used to describe All That Is. If your image of God is strictly male-oriented, or you have resistance to it, consider what creates meaning for you in that word. Reflect on which words denote a more masculine or a more feminine aspect of God for you, and why. In this book, I will use several different words, and all refer to the same loving, nurturing, radical love that is the All. Be aware of the voice of resistance, and the voice that accepts some words and rejects others. Healing with the words is often a healing of relationships that introduced a conditional, unkind God when you were a child. It may even be a healing of your relationship to the Divine.

As you enter the journey into this book and try out the practices suggested, there will be blocks that arise or times when you, for no apparent reason, want to give up or give in. Notice the voices within that want you to give up or give in. Later in this book we will look at ways to be with these voices so that they do not become you and your future and present are not controlled by them.

This awareness has kept me dedicated to spiritual practice and has kept me in awe that some of the most profound lessons in life are the most simple. With this in mind, I offer you two helpful reminders to continue to develop spiritual discipline: Practice and Divine Timing. Write these words on individual post-it notes and place at eye level in areas where you're not just passing by, remembering instead to look, contemplate and act on them.

In many ways, the discipline of spiritual practice is the same as any other practice. When I first learned to amplify my voice when speaking publicly, I was highly aware of pushing the sound out and of breathing properly. Having a naturally soft voice, I thought this task would be near impossible. Little by little the soft voice turned into a strong voice, and the strong voice became my voice. This practice that leads to non-trying and non- willpower is a return to the heart of love, a remembrance of who you are.

Divine Timing is the reminder that a spiritual lesson tends to surface when you are meant to receive it. There are lessons I wish I had received earlier and wonder why I didn't. Yet, I believe that part of my journey is to learn to sit with the mystery and the not-knowing. To surrender and not try to force something to happen. To learn to not need a reason for why things happen as they do. This is not what women are taught in patriarchal society. Often, the Divine Feminine wisdom teachings present themselves when nothing appears to be happening—when there is no visible transformation. Love this part of your journey as much as you love the transformations.

At times, you may go through a dark night of the soul, where you feel that no support exists; that you are completely alone. I remember in my darkest hour, asking for support and wondering why I wasn't getting any. Suddenly in my mind's eye I saw Jesus with a walking stick. Instead of having a sturdy, flat bottom surface for support, this stick had a series of different-sized roots coming out from the bottom; making it useless to lean on. What I understood from this image is that the roots we establish, all the relationships, material things, our home, country and belief systems, are a source of support that is actually a grand illusion. It may seem to our intellect and five senses that these provide our support—yet there is death, there is divorce, there is financial upheaval, there is a severing of close relationships. Like the walking stick Jesus showed me, the "roots" are useless to lean on.

The support we have cannot always be seen because we haven't trained ourselves to see with different eyes. God comes to us in ways that our mind cannot comprehend. Your body knows this and feels the Divine imbue it with love. Sometimes it is solely a feeling, other times, your support peeks through the eyes of a stranger, the conversation of lovers, the tear on your cheek, the bridge from your head to your heart and from your heart to that of another. It is the brief meeting of two souls destined to be called together to remember they are not alone. Support that is at once an instant and an eternity.

Throughout the pages of this book, I have included some of my most personal journal writings that best illustrate the processes, insights and exercises. In order to retain their authentic heart nature, they are not edited. They also stand as an example of my human nature: I too am on this Divine Feminine path with challenges and frustrations that arise. One of these challenges is that I spent most of my life in masculine modes of thinking, acting and feeling. I idolized the male essence because in my generation, society taught girls that being masculine was our best choice at "success".

JOURNAL INSIGHTS: ONE WOMAN'S CALLING

"There was no other option for me
than to move toward my true nature."
Elizabeth Lesser (quoting workshop participant)
author of *Broken Open: How Difficult Times Help Us Grow*

I am sitting in the backyard of a complete stranger, listening to a waterfall and wondering how I ended up here, alone, without my children, without a partner to take a happily-ever-after vacation.

The logical reason is that I am here to finish writing this book, to finally have the time away from all earthly responsibility to go where few women have gone before—where no time exists and all that is presented before me is the blank page and the stillness of the Ashland, Oregon air on an early summer morning.

My soul breathes uneasiness into this assumption, as I feel the urge to run back to my former identity, to rest easy in the traditions of family; even my aging mother is left alone as I sit here and "finish the book".

The guilt of duty and moral obligation seep into my body and I struggle to stop the tears. I swallow; I push down the feeling that rises within my body and hear the words of a wise mentor, Anne Marie Wright, who told me that tears are the orgasm of the heart. Go with them. I refuse to release.

My mind then searches for a society approved reason for being here—takes me back to the "logical side" of the book, the intellectual arguments about Mary and the Divine Feminine. This is a safe place to be, posing questions and hypothesis, dissecting concepts and challenging traditions. This is the "me" that I can identify with. My guilt begins to lessen as I attach myself to the role of Karen the Scholar. Now she has a reason to be here, to be away from loved ones, a focus away from loss and pain and guilt.

I breathe deeply and am about to begin this safe writing, when the "orgasm" begins again and this time I cannot stop it. My body shakes to expel the tears; my mind empties of everything except the deep feelings of sadness, loss and disappointment at the unbearable humanness within me.

When I return to my mind and feel the clearing of my heart, I suddenly know what I must do. It is no longer an option. I must tell my story, yes for my healing, yes for personal insight, and then for the calling I cannot afford to ignore any longer: to be a conduit of heart opening; of the discovery of the gentleness of the heart; of the Divine Feminine wisdom found in the body, in the spirit, and not outside of self.

I invite you to discover the Madonna Code within. It is a journey of remembrance of your Divine Feminine heart. Celebrate that which you are. Nurture it, understand it and give it to a world that so desperately needs it. The time is now. Your actions, your thoughts, your feelings, matter. In the mystical way of the feminine, all is one.

1

THE HEART OF VIRGIN LOVE

TAKE YOURSELF BACK to the serenity of Mother Earth. Imagine the aquamarine waters of a pristine lake surrounded by mountains and lush green forests. At the base of the mountains, emerging from the trees, is a barefoot woman in a simple cotton dress. She breathes in rhythm with her slow and sure-footed step. Sinking her toes into the warm earth at water's edge, she extends one large belly-breath and a smile.

What feelings are you aware of as you see this image in your mind? What words come to you?

Release this image and let the feelings dissolve. Now say the word "virgin". What thoughts and emotions do you associate with this word? How much of what you are thinking or feeling is based on societal norms, media and marketing, religion, or other aspects of your personal experience and upbringing?

My own reflection on these questions and visualization arise from the disconnect between woman in her natural state of being, Mother Nature as the ultimate expression of being, and the word "virgin". Institutions and their media love language and labeling as a means to influence and persuade. And I had fallen under their spell. To me, virgin was what popular women's magazines were trying to sell... a pure, innocent and *very* young woman... the ideal we all should seek to either be or be with. Every part of my body and mind resisted this ideal, yet it became my definition of virgin.

Under this spell of illusion, I resisted writing as I struggled to understand the virgin aspect of Mary. I kept a cool distance when contemplating it, unable to bring it to my deeper heart and feel the passion of its essence. Ironically, the root meaning of the biblical term for virgin (bethulah) is "separated". Although I honored Mary, the emphasis on her physical virginity was the isolating aspect of a woman I longed to embrace as a human and Divine Mother.

Many of my friends also felt the separation of the literal virgin and self. Deep uneasiness surrounded our discussions of Mary as virgin; beliefs or disbeliefs about Mary's status as a virgin were challenged and debated. Some pointed out that her own birth, through her elderly mother Anne, was Divine conception, making both mother and son deities on Earth. Others refused to acknowledge the possibility of a virgin birth. And then there were those who were adamant that Mary, after her virgin birth, went on to have more children, generating the "eternal virgin" or the "one-time" virgin debate.

I now believe that fixation on Mary's literal virginity has, over time, eroded relationships with her as the embodiment of Divine Feminine wisdom and love. The relationship to Mary as woman has been minimized by

Western civilization's repression of women's sexuality. The emphasis on Mary's eternal virginity separates her from women, as she is placed in a golden cage, where adoration of the Virgin is literal and intellectual, keeping us at a safe distance, mere observers of the Sacred Feminine. And as long as we continue to be observers, we cannot make the fundamental shift to the sacred heart of her unconditional (or as I call it) radical love.

Another word I have always been uncomfortable with is "pure", because it strikes me as a word of judgment that categorizes women according to how they behave. However, as I listen to the wisdom of Marianne Williamson, Andrew Harvey and many others, they speak of a different purity—that of the Sacred Feminine Heart. This is the Heart that flows, accepts and loves from moment to moment, surrendering attachment to an ego-based world.

In his awe-inspiring book, *Mary's Vineyard: Daily Meditations, Readings and Revelations*, Andrew Harvey quotes Reshad Field, who shares a similar perspective of the purity of the virgin:

> The Blessed Virgin was chosen to bear the prophet Jesus because she kept her purity intact. Ordinary people refer to this as keeping her virginity, but those beings with the grace of deeper understanding know that to be pure means to flow completely with each moment, fully adaptable, to become like a ceaseless river, cascading from the very waters of life itself.

Mary's life was so filled with new and challenging experiences that she seemed to be always in the realm of "first time". From her pregnancy to fleeing with her baby, to mothering, to surrendering, to the resistance against her son, to the violence of the crucifixion, to continuing the message and healing; hers was a constantly shifting world. What is remarkable about her story is that despite living in a state of not knowing, despite the constant upheavals, her openhearted being was free of judgment and expectation—she lived as compassionate love from moment to moment.

SACRED PRACTICE

In a journal, record your perception of the word purity. Write down all your beliefs and assumptions about it. Now, sit quietly and let go of everything you just wrote. Feel into your heart, breathe from that space and then focus on the feeling of purity. Where is it in your body? Does it feel light or heavy, clear or cloudy, bright or dim, colorful or colorless? Now go back to your journal and record your sensations. Are these words aligned with your original list that defined purity? If not, why might this difference exist? There is no need to try to fix or change; this is simply an exercise in awareness.

MYSTERY AND THE VIRGIN VICTORY

Sometimes, Divine Chaos is necessary to return us to our Virgin Heart—the heart that is comfortable with not knowing; the heart that flows with what is. When I turned forty and watched as the world meticulously planned began to crumble, I felt as though I was suddenly thrown into a soap opera where vast, devastating change was about to strike at any moment. During the space of a few weeks, while my husband and I separated, I also separated from my two closest friends and business partners, and one of my children spent the summer in hospital. While caring for my son, surrounded by the ill and injured, repressed memories of childhood trauma began to surface. I could not have orchestrated such vast change and synchronistic timing had I spent my lifetime doing it. Divine Chaos called me forth and brought me mercilessly to another realm of reality that no longer fit with who I thought I was, the roles I played and where my life was headed.

In this void, where comfort and structure are stripped away, is the space of the not-knowing—the space I least wanted to be in, and the one I most needed to experience. It is where I first discovered the Eternal Virgin; beginning fresh each moment, trusting the vast and infinite Sacred Heart.

The not-knowing led me to tasting the freedom of the Madonna Code—it unlocked the remembrance of who I am. By losing everything that defined me, I found what had never been lost, only veiled.

To live in the Divine and to be human, is to live in paradox. During my fortieth year, the face of tragedy was also the face of victory. In meditation, I heard a voice say, "Life is not a game or competition, but if you feel you must win, win that which is unknowable." Now I understand the profound meaning of this trust in the space of the unknown. It is the Virgin's essence; the glorious victory of the Virgin.

Feel back to a time in your life when your world was utter chaos and you didn't know from week to week how your life would "turn out". Perhaps on the one hand, you felt great stress and the desire to control your outcome.

You wanted people to act a certain way, events to reveal themselves on your terms. On the other hand, you may have released your stronghold on your future life plans and opened to the present; you marveled, if only for a moment, at Divine Chaos and its gifts of surrender and trust. You were aware of the opportunity to return to a more authentic self, stripped of knowing, certainty and structure. In the midst of your deepest challenge, you may have made a conscious decision (at least for a moment) to return to your essential Virgin nature, what Marion Woodman calls the Virgin Archetype: "That aspect of the feminine, in man or in woman, that has the courage to Be and the flexibility to be always Becoming."

Part of this embodiment of Becoming is our acceptance of the Sacred Feminine As Mystery. Patriarchal values aim to defeat mystery and claim knowledge over it. Yet it is the full embodiment of it that is the essence of the Virgin Within. It runs its wild course despite patriarchal insistence on knowing all and using the knowledge to make order and sense of the world.

While reading Natalie Goldberg's *Old Friend from Far Away: The Practice of Writing Memoir*, I was struck by one of the activities, which was to reflect on the question: "What could I give up knowing?" My immediate answer was "myself". With this intuitive response, I realized there are two forms of knowledge: one acquired through the intellect and used by the ego, the knowledge that often results in the story of me, you, us. And because it is just a story, it isn't real. This knowledge comes and goes with my thoughts and feelings. The second form of knowledge, spiritual wisdom, is the experience by which I come to know who I really am. It is the process within *The Madonna Code*, the experience of divinity, the knowledge of eternal truth. This truth is what the ego is least interested in and will resist at all costs. No-ing is the ego's job. Knowing Truth is the soul's job.

THE VIRGIN HEART

The Virgin Heart, when fully embodied, is the Heart that trusts in the Truth. It opens to people again and again because it knows that only love is real; it knows that regardless of other's words or actions, the truth of love is immovable. Because of this deep knowing, the Virgin Heart becomes a power that is foreign to most people—it is the power of the innocent; it is the Universal Divine Feminine love that infiltrates every cell of every being. It exists without judgment, expectation, or assumption. It retains the mystical virgin quality of complete trust in the truth of love.

In many ancient sacred texts and recent spiritual and channeled materials, Mary is seen as a woman who understands the Truth of love. From a very young age, she lived the Virgin Heart within the context of oppression, rejection and violence. Throughout the centuries, the boundaries of religion and the repression of women in patriarchal society have not scathed this authentic purity. As Andrew Harvey says in *The Return of the Mother*, Mary is beyond the moral and ethical controls that have been placed in society because her love is so pure: "Hers is the purity of total love, the purity of the desire that rises from total love to see all of her children illuminated and whole in the ground of ordinary life, fully divine and fully human, with nothing left out and nothing left unlit by the truth of love." This all encompassing love freely emanates from the Virgin Heart. It is this Heart that will create a world full of the Pregnant Virgin.

In *Mary's Vineyard*, Harvey quotes Rumi, who presents us with this image: "The universal soul met a separate soul/And placed a pearl on her breast/Through such a touch, the soul, like Mary,/Became pregnant with a heart ravishing messiah."

In our deepest heart, we are all pregnant with this messiah. We can desire this experience of impregnation, yet resist it simultaneously. Through years of adopted beliefs, we deny the messiah within and separate from our divinity. The birth of Christ Consciousness remains a seed buried deep within the wisdom of our heart-womb. And yet every woman intuitively knows that in sitting with her heart she waters the seed. In leaving her mind to rest, she bathes the seed in nutrients. In trusting the act of being with her feminine divinity, she invites Life to blossom.

JOURNAL INSIGHTS: SITTING WITH MY HEART

The truth is that I can, as many creative people do, get caught up in the brilliance of my own mind, in the subtleties of my own thoughts and words, and so begin the charade of covering up what I really know to be true, and what I am really feeling at a deep level.

I've heard the Voice over the past few months clearly say, "Leave everything behind and follow me." I knew this to be what Jesus told the fishermen who later became his disciples, yet for me, the message was about moving from the complexity of my mind to the simplicity of my heart. The idea of sitting with the sadness of my heart was unbearable and I was doing everything I could to escape it, including philosophical and spiritual contemplation.

Crying, I've come to realize, isn't the greatest expression of sadness, the kind of grief I'm talking about. It's like elementary school for healing. Yet sitting still in my heart, which has no words, no form, scares me. The lack of structure is the uncontrolled, all encompassing touch of God: the Divine Feminine in its full, wild beauty.

It is simplicity at its core.

The truth today is that I mourn the young woman I was. The one who had "it" figured out and thought "it" would be unchanged. Until "it" was at her feet, and where to start? What piece to pick up?

I want to cradle them all, these pieces, like holding the newborn baby who can't and won't be consoled. I want to hold those screams and tears until we both collapse from sheer exhaustion into a deep sleep.

And what I want most is to awaken from this pain, yet the only way I can do this is to go through it, not around it.

So today, I choose to sit with my heart. A Princess looks for her heart to be rescued. A Queen reclaims it with Truth. And sometimes Truth, in all her beauty, is shown most fully through the unreasonable voice of wisdom, the unthinkable act of Being: "Leave everything behind and follow me".

SEPARATION AND THE VIRGIN CHALLENGE

The importance of heart-based wisdom is that it does not separate mind, body and spirit. Fear-based beliefs and assumptions, however, are the ego mind's "wisdom". When I began sitting with my heart and experiencing the love of the Divine, Mary presented me with a disturbing vision of a body that was neatly separated into parts. She explained that beliefs, thoughts and actions that separate us from the whole of ourselves also separate us from our Sacred Feminine. It is the Sacred Feminine that unifies everything in its acceptance and love: body and spirit, heart and mind, sexuality and the sacred, humanity and divinity.

Patriarchal influence has suppressed the Virgin Heart because, for centuries, we have accepted the belief that it is natural to be ruled by fear and conflict. The vision of Mary tells me otherwise; this image of a body separated from itself is anything but natural. Imagine coming from a culture and family that believe our natural state to be one of peace and unity; a culture and family that experience enlightenment here on earth, within their earthly bodies and minds. In *The End of Your World: Uncensored Straight Talk on the Nature of Enlightenment*, author Adyshanti says that humans look for altered states of consciousness when seeking enlightenment yet humanity is already in an altered state of consciousness…separation!

Returning to the wholeness of the Virgin where separation is unnatural, is a collective challenge as much as it is an individual one. One collective challenge is language itself. Language limits us by creating structure for labeling an experience, idea, event, or person. Once something is given a label it fits neatly into a particular belief and this belief can lead to fear-based thoughts that keep us from being fully present and united with our Divinity.

The self-help industry of the past two decades has brought a certain level of consciousness to the collective yet it has missed the mark with some of the language chosen to describe concepts. One such concept is "self" love. The Virgin Heart knows nothing of "self" love, which suggests separateness and a love that is different from love of another. As the Virgin Heart lives moment to moment, surrendering to the giving and receiving of radical love, it has no concept of self love; rather, it simply knows and feels this love as the foundation of life itself. And it is in living the Sacred Feminine wholeness that limiting words need not exist. After all, who are you when you contemplate whether you love yourself enough? What happens to your energy field? Is it strong, or does it grow weak? When you contemplate self-love, who is the "I" that is doing that contemplating? What if the "I" dissolved into the arms of the Sacred Feminine and began to feel the wholeness again? What would your world look like, feel like?

Human beings use language to find personal meaning, to create identity and to feel worthy. Imagine if there were no words for "successful", "kind", "wealthy", "generous", "motivated", "charismatic"; no words for "unworthy", "mean", "stupid", "incapable" and "unreliable"; no words to hang our identity on? I believe that we would freely allow feelings to just show up and leave. Our thoughts would be less likely to turn into the Velcro voices that insist that we, or others, are this or that.

If you refrain from immediately using language to label something, define it, condemn it, or praise it, and instead simply enter the present moment, you will realize the sacredness of Life and feel it in your body and around you. You become the sacredness of Life.

Nature is a great teacher of the silent, languageless Now. Eckhart Tolle, in *Stillness Speaks,* describes this ultimate virgin symbol and the use of language that diminishes it:

Watch an animal, a flower, a tree and see how it rests in Being. It is itself. It has enormous dignity, innocence and holiness. However, for you to see that, you need to go beyond the mental habit of naming and labeling. The moment you look beyond mental labels, you feel that ineffable dimension of nature that cannot be understood by thought or perceived through the senses. It is a harmony, a sacredness that permeates not only the whole of nature but is also within you.

Surrendering to this space of no language, no thought, brings the Divine Feminine Virgin back to our being. As we are intimately one with Nature, Nature the Great Virgin, becomes one with us. The silence of a single moment—the awe, the reverie, the gazing that becomes one with the universe, shifts the moment a word is uttered. The named experience then must be acted on; the unnamed experience is the moment when your entire body, your whole being, is here Now. Being completely present *is* Divine Love and your Virgin Heart can experience it at any moment.

FUSION OF BODY AND SPIRIT

For most of my adult life, I did not feel God as the sacred harmony of the Divine Feminine and Masculine within me but as a conceptual understanding accessed through my intellect. Even as I began to read sacred texts and discover more of the world's spiritual rituals and disciplines, I never "got" the feeling of the Divine as an in-body experience. I had experienced mystical awakenings outside my body yet

I had no recognition that this same experience could take place within my body.

My curiosity about the body as a Chalice for Spirit grew as I connected with teachers, circles and workshops that opened my heart to the possibility and experience of it. The Chalice was foreign and strangely familiar at the same time. During one workshop, I met a teacher who talked of the experience of the Observer, who serves as the detached voice of acceptance and love for what is, regardless of what is going on in life. It is the ego-buster because it defuses the ego energy through this loving observation and acceptance. When I told this teacher of one of my mystical, out-of-body experiences and likened it to the Observer experience, I was shocked when he stood silent looking into my eyes and gently said, "Bring the Observer into your body." I wondered if that was even possible.

I learned that the honoring of my body is connected deeply with the way in which I experience or don't experience the Sacred Feminine. At a subconscious level, I had taken on a belief that my body was not worthy of the radical love of the Divine, so the only way I could access it was to go outside my body.

For some people, prayer is also an out-of-body experience, as it is projected "out there" and not felt within the heart and depths of the body. In many religions, control of the body and a full or partial vacating of the body is encouraged. This often causes people to deny the wisdom of their body; the holistic prayer of the Virgin Heart becomes fragmented.

In *The Feminine Face of God*, Anderson and Hopkins interview Carol Collopy, a spiritual teacher, who spent a lifetime praying and meditating. In meditation one day, she heard a voice say, "Do not lift your prayers out of your body. Give up everything that is outside the body." Carol was shocked by this suggestion, yet years later, experienced it as a profound shift in her intimacy with the Divine and in the physical healing of the cancer within her body.

This is where Mary as Virgin is critical for women: Mary's body is the representation of our bodies, completely penetrated by Spirit. We are impregnated with the radical love of Spirit. Mary's body was the human Chalice for Spirit, the Womb of Consciousness. We have the opportunity to claim our human body as a chalice for Sacred Feminine wisdom and love. And this can begin through conversation or prayer within the body.

Sacred Practice

As you begin your prayer, notice where it is directed to. Is there an energetic flow outside your body or inside? If inside, where do you feel the prayer? If you have difficulty feeling the prayer within, try focusing on your heart and with each breath, imagine that your heart is swelling with love as you either remain silent or use words. This heart expansion then moves to other parts of your body, radiating love. Soon you will feel the freedom of this type of prayer as it lifts you into the presence of love.

RECEIVING BODY LOVE

Because the Virgin lives fully as Life, without the ego need to separate, the flow of love for self and another is infinite and unimpeded. While the Mother Heart is giving the Virgin Heart is receiving. In meditation, many of my own conversations with Mary return to her gentle suggestion: "Love your body." I realized that I could not fully receive from another or love myself if I did not honor and love my body.

The practice of honoring our bodies is a sacred one and goes beyond physical care to a spiritual infusion of Mother Love. This is the ultimate body care and the least practiced. Some women spend small fortunes beautifying and relaxing their bodies at spas yet have no inner experience of love within their bodies. The result of this is a body that never heals; it is a body that is fed the seeming "goddess treats" on the outside yet is empty on the inside. It is a body that suffers from lack of love.

Marion Woodman, in *The Pregnant Virgin: A Process of Psychological Transformation*, talks about the necessity of reclaiming the body: "Unless the body knows that there are inner loving arms strong enough to contain it, however fierce or broken it may be, it will hang onto its own rigidity in an effort to survive."

Women's bodies need love. This love may come from an outside source but the sustaining love of the Inner Arms comes from the body-spirit connection.

For many women, the idea of receiving these Inner Arms through the body is challenging, either based on personal experiences of body and heart violation, or simply by being part of a culture in which the body has been devalued or dismissed as insignificant. We live in a time where many of us are beginning to realize that the sacred is not reserved for a special few; the sacred is here now, within and around us. It is in all of our bodies, hearts and spirits. Because we rarely feel this collectively we have little experience of our sacred body uniting with sacred practice.

Negative body perception has resulted in shame or unworthiness connected to our bodies or projected onto the bodies of others. These feelings result in habits of compartmentalizing the body into individual objects to be evaluated, compared, judged. Even praise of one part of the body leads to comparison with another part. And so the Whole Virgin becomes the disembodied, "tainted" Other who is never accepted in the deepest core of self.

SACRED PRACTICE

Practice receiving Divine Love. Because She, our Divine Mother, is grounded in the body of the earth and in our bodies, she can be found waiting for us there within, at any and every moment in time. Sit quietly and ask Her to bring waves of love or warmth and light through your body. Feel the movement of the Sacred Feminine the moment you ask, as it is instantaneous. Remember to ask and release any expectations of what the experience will be. Stay open to receiving this love.

Connecting to the Virgin Body

If Nature is the ultimate Virgin, then our views of it would ideally parallel views of self. Yet this is rarely the case. As we see beauty in a mountain, stream, ocean, we can look into the mirror and see the beauty of our body as a whole. Just as it would seem absurd to dissect a stream, waterfall, or mountain, it would be equally strange to claim that one part of the body is acceptable and worthy of love while another is not. Feel the body as sacred, beautiful, awe-inspiring—*as it is.*

In returning to Mother Nature, feeling and honoring her, we also feel and honor our deepest feminine essence and our body. Through immersion in our six senses, we feel the Virgin in a powerful, instinctual way in a simple, mindful walk in a forest, or along a stream. Taking off shoes and walking barefoot is a simple reminder to connect our bodies with the sacred ground beneath us that sustains and supports us. It keeps Divine Feminine energy visceral and reminds us of the ever-present moment of Now…the ultimate state of the Virgin.

Sacred Practice

Listen to your body—the wise guide that keeps you on track with feeling your connection to the Sacred Feminine. Record your body's pains, vital energy and lack of responsiveness, joy, or any other sensations, as you go about your day. Ask yourself: Is my body telling me that I am remembering who I am, or is it telling me that I am indulging in who I am not?

Remembrance of who we are is often so at odds with corporate and government structures that when we at last recognize who we are not, we are guided back to the voice of the heart, leading a new generation of spiritual seekers. This return to truth can be observed in your body, so keeping a journal of the sacred temple of truth—your body—will keep you aware and focused.

MEDITATIVE REFLECTIONS FOR THE VIRGIN HEART

- ♥ Open at every moment to what Is. Here you will find your Virgin Heart, wild and free.

- ♥ Your body as Chalice fills with Love's Truth. It is happening right now. Can you feel it?

- ♥ Your Sacred Heart is calling you to release meaning and invite experience.

2

Presence and the Virgin Heart

Journal Insights: Do you believe in magic?

As I browse through the books of a metaphysical store in Ashland, Oregon, I am intrigued by a young man wandering about the books and giftware. He is quite possibly the most joyful person I've come across in a long time. He calls himself Curly and he is a magician from England. He has dreadlocks and a sparkle in his eyes that brings curiosity to everyone he talks to, and he talks to everyone in the store. I see that he carries a sizeable backpack and am aware that it contains everything he owns. I hear him ask the store clerk if she has ever seen a unicorn. She giggles nervously and says that no, she has never seen one because they don't exist. He laughs uproariously and says, "Indeed they do exist, I saw one in Northern Alberta. I've also seen fairies on a number of occasions." She smiles and says, "That's nice dear," and goes back to rearranging the giftware.

He browses for a few minutes more, commenting on the music, the colors, every sense and detail presented to him. He notices all of it and joyfully celebrates. I hear him say that he currently lives in British Columbia and just visited the North Country Fair in Alberta to perform his magic shows. I grew up in the area where the Fair takes place and now live in the province of British Columbia, so I acknowledged our connection. Looking in his eyes, I instantly recognize a person that came to earth for the specific reason of helping people live in the moment of joy and awe and wonder. His presence is infectious and the whole room fills with joy as he mingles around, singing and noticing all the delights around him.

I think, "Wouldn't it would be great for him to speak at one of my spiritual events?" so I ask him for his contact information. He says, "I have a name. Curly. I don't have a way for you to contact me, but you will find me everywhere." His words rang through my body and I instantly knew my soul had just received a profound message. "I don't have a way for you to contact me, but you will find me everywhere."

If we search for Presence, if we go after it as a goal or intention, we will not find it. It is not contactable; it doesn't live in the concrete, reasonable world of the mind. The paradox is that it can be found everywhere, at every moment in time. All we need is to merge with this moment in complete trust and surrender; then we become the love that exists there.

Curly is the love that exists in the moment.

Curly casually walks out the door, leaving us all in a magical reverie, and as I pay for my items the cashier says, "I want to know his secret. I looked at his eyes and he's not on drugs." I said nothing, wanting to keep the moment in a sacred silent space, until writing about it now. I knew what his secret was. And he was spreading it like wildfire for those who were ready.

WOMEN, PRAYER AND BEING HERE NOW

Curly exemplified the Virgin Heart of present moment awareness; his energy is a spark that stays with me even as I write this book. A few days after he left I returned to the Ashland metaphysical store and skimmed through books about how to be in the present moment, yet few spoke to my heart as a woman. While I didn't know it at the time, I was searching for something that would guide, support, love and nurture my tender heart and bring it back to its full strength. Deep down I had lost the capacity to do this for myself and hoped that some of these books would act as guides to heal my broken heart. I was searching for a feminine way to bring me home to being here now.

In my search, I realized that I had already experienced an ancient form of Presence. During a retreat for women, held by women's circle facilitator Nancy Kerner, I experienced the power of women praying together in circle. Nancy invited us into our hearts and the hearts of all the women around us by asking each of us to hold a thread of yarn connected to every other woman. We whispered our prayers at the same time, and I could feel the unity of love, the Divine Feminine carried through the threads, merging together until nothing else existed but the sound of prayers. I was completely surrounded by and imbued with the sacred.

Soaking up the truth of the Divine Feminine is like having a glorious bath with wonderful aromatic oils that soothe and nurture the skin, versus a harsh shower that strips the skin of its natural oils. It is in this warmth that I began to contemplate the nature of prayer and how women were told (and in many cases threatened) for thousands of years to take prayer outside of self and to experience it much like a victim who needs and wants something in order to survive. This form of prayer was most common as I began my descent into the mystery of my fortieth year; I knew of no other way but to beg and plead for an outcome that would make me feel safe, secure and loved. Yet Spirit, in its wonderful all-knowing, led me to a completely different space—the one that would change my relationship with Her as a silky bath can change our experience of water.

My first discovery came from my beloved Poor Clare's, the monastic nuns of St. Claire of Assisi, whose soul and sole purpose is to be immersed in prayer. They taught me that prayer does not need to be in words; it may be the state of being in which you go about your day. Gardening, (they are self sufficient for much of the year with a large garden) with complete attention to the soil and plants, is a form of prayer. Gratitude for the sun and breeze as they tend to the garden is a form of prayer. This form of prayer, I realized, is what had been missing my whole life—the present moment prayer that needs nothing and wants nothing. It simply exists as the love that we are made of.

In entering the Virgin moment, the present moment, we enter a sacred prayer, the one that whispers to our very souls and universe: I trust you, I trust Life and I know I am one with it. This prayer brings an understanding that peace is the essence of the natural world. A flower basks in the glorious sun, opening its petals to vibrant love energy without asking why the sun bathes its body or what happens when the sun goes down at night or the clouds settle in for a storm. If we can experience being part of this natural world from moment to moment, we become that peace. We become one with our Virgin Heart.

This takes great practice and commitment and may seem formidable at times; yet if you can choose only one single practice to bring you into the Virgin moment, this alone will be enough. One of my favorite prayers of Presence is to simply feel one of the many qualities of love without attaching any meaning to the environment around me, the people, or the events. The feeling always is centered in now, not on memories of the past or hopes for the future, because I find that if I engage in that, my mind takes me away to anything but Presence.

Sacred Practice

A process I take my workshop participants into involves cultivating moments in the day where they become aware of the love feeling that wants to express itself through them. You can do this at home by taking a few minutes to allow the energy of this love to fill your body. The energy can be any form of love, such as peace, joy, compassion, awe and many others. You may identify with a particular feeling of love that is nameless. There is no need to put a label on it, for as you name something, the mind wants to categorize and explore it. In the Presence Prayer, it is best to simply feel it and through this feeling, come to know your feminine divinity.

While I was at a peace sanctuary in Mount Shasta, California, I walked a labyrinth which had as its center a tiny statue of Mary and some offerings that people had left Her. When I came to that center, I knelt down and bowed my head, asking to feel her Presence. The moment my request left my lips, a powerful, warm, light-filled bubble of energy surrounded my body and I knew that this form of prayer where I could feel every ounce of the Divine, was exactly what she wanted to show me. In the remainder of the labyrinth, I set the intention to know what love is and kept hearing the guidance, "Feel it" repeatedly. If there can be only one practice for women to get their bodies connected with Divine Feminine essence, it is this.

I also believe that a form of prayer is to feel everything that is not love, fully and completely. This is a prayer of release, a prayer of surrender, a prayer of trust. Sometimes, this prayer is the only thing that saves a closed heart, bringing it back to love. But for many people, an exercise in feeling is avoided at all costs because it usually comes with unwanted emotion. When I knelt before Mary at the center of the labyrinth, I could feel a strong pull of energy come out of my mouth as though my body wanted to scream and I had not allowed it to. She was showing me that I had the residue of pain in my body that wanted to be released so that I could come to clarity, forgiveness and compassion for myself and for others. With Divine timing I discovered *Women, Food and God,* opening it to a page where author Geneen Roth encourages a similar process: "In the process of resisting the emptiness, in the act of turning away from our feelings…we ignore what could utterly transform us. But when we welcome what we most want to avoid, we evoke that in us that is not a story, not caught in the past, not some old image of ourselves. We evoke divinity itself."

SACRED PRACTICE

Another embodiment of this essence is to use the breath to begin your Presence Prayer, focusing entirely on being here Now, versus going to your intellect to discuss or ask for things related to your future or past. As you breathe in a deep belly breath and exhale until all of the air has been expelled, feel your body begin to relax and ground itself into the earth. You may wish to feel your bare feet on soil as you do this, to have the sensory connection with the earth. Now with each inhale, imagine every cell of your body radiating a warm, loving light (use whatever color intuitively comes to you) that you feel in every part of your body. Imagine that this light begins to extend a few inches beyond your body. Each time as you breathe in, imagine that this light is extending further and further, and with each exhale it is reaching out beyond you to your loved ones in your home, to your neighbors, community, world community and into the heavens. You feel one with this light, you are this light. You are the blessing, the miracle. Feel this truth as your radiant energy bathes the world with love. Stay with this Virgin moment of truth until you are ready to return and slowly wiggle your toes and fingers, open your eyes and affirm that you are the miracle, you are the love that you have been searching for.

THE LANGUAGE OF PRAYER

While present moment prayer is powerful without language, it can also incorporate words that are focused, concise and intended to stimulate the energy of love. The words can be radiated out into the world, but when you are beginning this form of prayer, allow it to stay centered within, flowing into your heart and soul, connecting with the Sacred Feminine through your sacred body.

Find the words that deeply resonate with your spirit. For some, the words may be all those associated with qualities of love, for others, they may be the many names of God, great spiritual masters, or angels. When I would visit the Poor Clares, one of the nuns told me to simply say the name "Jesus" over and over as a form of prayer. I also find that saying the name "Mary" is a powerful focusing prayer that fills my body with the energy of love. When I attended a women's circle and together we chanted the word "love", I could feel my body vibrate with the essence of love and heard a ringing in my ear (which I believe to be the message of angels). You may repeat a mantra from your spiritual tradition. With whatever method you choose, know that each is a form of prayer that gives you a portal, or entrance into the present moment of Spirit. If you don't feel anything and you find yourself wishing you did, drop all expectations of an outcome. When you begin a spiritual practice the most vital aspect of maintaining it is to be detached from that practice giving you something. Do the practice for the sake of your relationship to Self and Spirit.

Asking and Being Here Now

Doreen Virtue often reminds her students of Angel Therapy Certification Courses to ask the angels for help because they cannot intervene if they are not asked. And I agree that there are times when we need to reach out and ask for help; when we need extra support from our Divine Team of angels and Ascended Masters. When we ask with the certainty that every request is answered, that every plea is heard, we discover that we are continuously guided and supported. In order to really make this discovery we need to live in the present moment and feel, hear, see and know this loving guidance.

What I do find curious is that when I am Here Now, it never occurs to me to ask for help, because in that space all is well. When we frequent the present moment, most often it is a heart-wisdom, a languageless responding rather than reacting, to the events around us. When we come from that Virgin Heart regardless of circumstance, we will taste the freedom that Jesus, Mary, Buddha and so many other spiritual leaders lived and shared with us.

Perhaps the danger in asking is that the mind demands a logical answer. And when the brain gets an answer that it cannot use reason to decode, it ignores the guidance or begins to diminish it or argue with it. Many intuitive messages are an affront to our mind and completely outrageous. I remember being told in the silence of my heart-wisdom to let go of a relationship in which I felt love and gave love to a degree never experienced before. Intellectually, I could see no reason to bring myself to do the unthinkable and sever the ties. Yet when I shared this information with my beloved, he admitted that he too had been feeling that we needed to part ways. I knew at that moment that if I chose to ignore the guidance I would then doubt every decision, whether it was based on intuition or not. I needed to follow through with the persistent voice and do the unthinkable.

I have learned that God is not reasonable and the big picture is not always mine to know and see. Imagine Mary being asked to be the mother of a Savior! Imagine if she had doubted what she saw and heard, and made the decision to deny the gift that was her life path. So if you ask, be open to hearing the truth and acting on it. The great healers throughout history could only begin the true journey of healing self and others the moment they fully received and acted upon the guidance of an Asking Prayer.

Another Asking Prayer is a request that serves others while developing our own spiritual qualities. For instance, when praying for peace, feel the peace within while sending the light of this peace to an area of the world where people are at war with themselves or others. When you are fully present in the moment, sending this light and simultaneously feeling it fill every cell of your body, you become the conduit of harmony within and around you. This strengthens loving co-creation with the Divine in a focused, intentional way that honors your capacity to be the change rather than the observer of change. I believe that we are never really an observer; we co-create that which is love-based or we co-create from fear, but we are never neutral bystanders.

THE VIRGIN MOMENT OF SACRED LOVE

In my own marriage, I was unaware of the importance of living in the present moment as it relates to intimacy and deeper soul connection. Both of us were individuals on separate journeys that never merged together to experience the sacredness of a moment, where we embodied Oneness. It's fascinating that the words used to sanctify marriage ceremonies in Christian tradition involve this unification: "Two shall become one." I believe that most of us live in illusion as to what that really means and why it is so vital to relationships.

I thought I had the perfect marriage because my husband and I were individual; we had our separate lives and did not feel the need to control each other. As a result, we rarely argued and felt fulfilled in our own paths. Yet after a decade of pursuing "the goal" of career achievement and supporting each other in doing so, I began to feel the isolation of the "two" and wanted the "one". This was not entirely on a conscious level; most of the time I could not express what was missing. And even when I recognized it, I didn't know how to take steps toward this oneness.

There comes a time in a conscious woman's life where she realizes that she never really loved. Yes a needy love, yes a transactional love, a love that warms her heart, even an erotic love filled with the opening of the passionate heart. But not the Divine Love she is. Not the love of the two shall become one. This realization breaks her heart and she encounters a host of illnesses: physical, emotional and mental. Sometimes she is released of an illness quickly, and sometimes it takes her years to come to the truth that heals.

This truth is found only here and now. The truth that you are the Divine Feminine that unifies all, brings together in harmony, gathers together the tribe of humanity. The truth that forms divine union with or without marriage. Join your beloved now in this moment; this is all that exists and it is all that you have together. Release your past together, release your pain, release your expectations and your goal to change the other, to change the relationship. Just be here now.

Growing up, most of us were aware that love was something that we felt when someone did or said something to win our hearts or we performed or whispered words in a way that caused us to feel appreciated and loved. In *The Return of the Feminine: Honoring Cycles of Nature*, author Dr. Rebecca Orleane notes that, "If we are focused on 'pleasing' or 'being pleased', we are not listening to the call to surrender necessary for holy union." I believe this call, this kiss, as I refer to it, is only found in the Virgin moment of now.

This is the kiss of the Romantic, not the mushy greeting card romance that is happy because your partner has fulfilled a need in you; it is the romance that exists because you have met here, in this moment. And here is where your love is boundless and borderless. Your love energies mix and twirl and dance with each other, until at last, like two clouds meeting in the sky, there is no distinction as the two surrender to the earth's forces that bring them into one.

Sacred Practice

Whether or not you are currently in a relationship, the heart-opening exercises below are an invitation to experience this unity.

- ♥ *Go for a hike or a swim out in nature. Feel every aspect of the sun, wind, water. Hear every noise of nature, see every leaf sway in the wind or fall to the ground; observe the waves of the water or the formation of rock as you tread gently on a trail. Saturate your senses and stay with them, being completely here, now. Do not talk or motion to your partner at all. After half-an-hour or so, rest with your partner and look into each other's eyes and hear the other breathing, see the color of their eyes, the gentle lines softening or dancing around their eyes, the fullness of their lips; feel with the tips of your fingers the loving texture of their skin, the veins in their hands and neck, the rhythm of their breath, the smell of their skin. See, smell, touch. Bring your awareness to all of your senses. As you taste the sweetness of the energy that begins to blend together you see your beloved in front of you no longer as him or her, but one body and soul. Your body and spirit do not begin or end, and your awareness of being One expands to all of Life around you. Together you become the truth that you are not separate. You never have been. Feel the truth of this love, the one love that you are, here, together, now.*

- ♥ *You can also experience the above exercise with a friend and practice the expansion of love energy and the blending of your energies so that you no longer feel separate from each other. Practice the art of indulging your five senses in nature and allow your body to receive nature's joy and peace. Feel your body become one with nature as you radiate love back into the earth, the wind, the trees, the water. Breathe into the* environment and let it fill you as you fill it; gradually two become one as you feel the bliss of this moment.

♥ Be *playful with your partner, as it naturally brings you straight into the present moment. Rather than specifically planning an activity, try leaving your home and going for a walk with the intention to be playful. Run, skip, climb, splash, be the child again. Grab a stick or pick a flower and discover how many ways each of you can create a game out of it. Become your authentic fun self, whether that is curious or wild or energetic, or full of zest, or whatever you choose. And then intentionally come together in this playful moment. Kiss with the energy that you are in that moment. Kiss with awe or curiosity. Kiss with excitement and energy. Kiss with wild abandon. Whatever the feeling, flow with it as you enter the kiss. Be in your body and your feelings without meaning-making. This is a time to feel the pleasure of being alive as One.*

♥ *Together with your partner experience being in service to others. Choose a single act of kindness to engage in. As you give of yourself bring your awareness to your heart and expand your energy to your partner's body. As each of you breathe out the energy of love feel the love that comes from each other and bring your awareness to its blending into one. Touch fingertips every few minutes as you work and know that this love energy you share is magnified and working in the community and world. The love of partners has an incalculable effect on Life; bringing much needed peace and joy. The more your beloved unites with you in service to others, the more your awareness of the Divine purpose of giving and receiving love saturates your knowing, your body, your soul.*

♥ *Service within a community that inspires you to Sacred Action is another way to connect on a deep level; as you work toward a common goal, practice feeling the unity of the group, the gratitude for the amplified power that a group brings to a project. This ignites Oneness and if you choose to enter a Sacred Romance, you may experience a deepening of connection, intimacy and joy never known before.*

The Presence of Isolation

One of the definitions of virgin is isolation—to be alone. Although the above exercises are done with a partner or friend, there is a tenderness and opening of the heart that often occurs when each partner retreats into isolation for a period of time. Women's circle facilitator, Nancy Kerner, knows that her relationship with her husband works best when she has the creative, intuitive, reflective time to herself that allows her to go deep within, to connect with her guidance, to uncover and discover. And men need this time too. It may look different and may not even be termed a retreat or inward focused activity, yet their time to part and return renewed, clear and energized is equally vital.

In *The Return of the Feminine*, Dr. Rebecca Orleane talks about women in indigenous cultures who take time out during their menstruation to honor the gifts of feminine cycles: intuition, body awareness, dreams and creativity. I believe that feminine cycles also offer women a time to leave their busy world behind and practice listening to their bodies and loving the power of their body to create, sustain life and be a vessel for our Divine purpose of open-hearted giving and receiving of love.

For much of my adult life, I have not been aware of my feminine cycles nor have I honored the instinctual messages to be quiet, retreat and go inward during my menstruation. I now believe this gift opens women more fully to the present time by asking them to pay attention to their bodies, the emotion that wants to express itself powerfully and the intuitive messages and dreams that arise. For the first time, I am now loving my menstruation as a time of Divine Feminine wisdom—a time to experience moment by moment the sacredness of the Miracle of the Body, Divine Guidance and union with Nature as the moon and tides flow with my cycles. This experience is what Mary has shown me—that separation from our nature takes us away from connection to Life. Presence during menstruation reaffirms that all is One.

I encourage women to retreat during their menstruation and invite young women to do the same. It can be devastating for young women to learn that a beautiful, natural and powerful aspect of being a woman is suppressed, ridiculed and dismissed by the majority of people they come in contact with. Most women, regardless of age, perceive the emotions they feel during this time as merely "hormonal". If women were taught to express fully all the emotions they are feeling and inquire into what might need to change, or what needs tending to, they would come to see their menstruation as an invaluable aspect of their feminine nature. With growing awareness of the benefits of isolation during menstruation, boys and men may appreciate the value of this cycle too and stop the degrading and belittling that too often damages our young women's concepts of what it means to be feminine.

This retreat need not be for days; even closing a door in your home and letting everyone know that this is your sacred time is a blessing. As you shift from being focused on the past and future, embracing a world where no-time and no-linear thinking exist; as you allow the flow of ideas, emotions, dreams, creativity and guidance to become one with your being; you will emerge as nature intended: having surrendered, released and renewed.

The process of menstruation is related to purity, as the word purification means to eliminate what is no longer needed. We can begin again in a new cycle. Women are always in the process of "beginning again"—the essence of the pure Virgin heart.

SACRED PRACTICE

♥ *Journal in isolation to express all that surrounds you in the moment. Avoid intellectualizing or playing with clever ideas. Simply pour your heart on paper. This is one heart-based action that you can share with a partner if both of you retreat and then unite again. It is in the coming together that you will build true connection and intimacy and co-create with the power of radical love.*

♥ *Before your next menstruation plan to take time out to rest and renew. Allow yourself to fully feel your body, dream, create and go into self. When you emerge from this time, notice how your body feels and how you enter the world again. Record these awarenesses.*

♥ *The feminine nature of retreat allows us to tap into healthy masculine energy as we emerge with clarity and wisdom, having listened to the truth and honored, loved and cared for our bodies and spirits. Notice how your masculine energy shifts when you emerge from retreat. Does it feel more in harmony with your feminine? Are they unified and co-creating?*

When I visit my beloved Poor Clares, I am reminded of the wisdom of isolation to keep constantly practicing being here now, in the Mother energy. When I watch the nuns tenderly weeding their garden or fervently praying alone in an outdoor chapel or quietly making tea and setting out a plate of cookies, I long for the simplicity of these acts. These women are so completely single-hearted (instead of single-minded) in whatever they do. This single-hearted being, this Virgin Presence, is easier in times of isolation where the business of life cannot intervene. I am writing this book, partly in isolation, as I know that my temptation is to call someone or e-mail or clean or organize; to find other projects and people to fill my time. Yet writing, like menstruation, is a time of deep inward contemplation; it demands I be here now and now and now. Cultivating a deep reverence for this time has helped me to emerge with insights and creativity that I now share with the women in my community and around the world. It is this inward movement and outward sharing that is the receiving and giving; it is the flow of love that is the essence of the Divine Feminine.

It was once common for women to menstruate with the dark of the moon, retreat and then emerge, sharing their insights with their community during the light of the moon. With technology and suppression of all that is natural, this is not as prevalent. But what has not been lost is the opportunity to unify with our community and to gather together in the light of our new beginnings, new insights, new creations. We are the facilitators of change in the world and it is time to honor that in every way and in every moment.

UNWANTED ISOLATION: THE VIRGIN MOMENT AND HEARTBREAK

When I experienced great loss in relationships, I found myself becoming needy for love, almost desperate for displays of affection, admiration and connection. The more I felt this neediness the more selfish I became and soon I was completely wrapped up in having my needs met without any gentleness and compassion for another. The odd thing was that I was aware of my behavior and completely unwilling to stop it! It was like witnessing a soap opera with drama that never ends unless you turn the TV off. But when I was finally ready to turn off the TV I couldn't find the switch.

If you are in the middle of the dark night of the soul and feel it is impossible to go through another day, know that you have an eternal light within that is infinitely more powerful than your egoic mind. You never have to look for the switch to this light because it is within you at all times. Remember it. Feel it. Know that you can experience miracles; your managed life *can* become a life magnified by the Divine within you.

Sacred Practice

First, feel with your entire body the extremes of your "what if" fears. List them all on paper, read them out loud and feel each of them fully. Open your body to them and allow yourself to surrender to this release in a safe and supportive environment. When you feel this is complete for now, (you may need to take these steps over and over throughout the day, week or month) mentally acknowledge and thank your mind for alerting you to your current perceptions and fears. As a third step, lay down in a quiet place, ideally in nature, and surround yourself with the peaceful energy of the ground beneath you and the sky above you, breathing deeply as you visualize your heart energy expanding beyond yourself into the air around you. Now with each person or event that you feel negative thoughts or emotions toward, focus your heart to be in service to that person, sending them your radical love energy. Your body was designed to be in service to Life; feel the truth of that and how it heals your sense of isolation as you give freely of this essence that is both you and the other. As you send this energy, dissolve into it so that there is no distinction between you and that person or people involved.

Stay with this feeling of loving service and know that you can re-create it anytime you wish. In a wonderful discussion with holistic health practitioner, Christine Kleiman, she shared with me how many women love to be of service to others, and if we can channel our passion for this into our intimate relationships, whether they are a current, past, or future love, we can find peace. Rather than the energy of fear (often fear of lack or unworthiness) that creates neediness and then selfishness, we can redirect that to produce the spiritual energy of radical love that sends love for the sake of being in service to Life, not for the sake of being acknowledged and rewarded. You may attempt to use such action in the hope of changing your loved one or receiving something you believe you need. This will only produce neediness because it is transactional love, an if/then form of love. Radical love, the essence of the Divine Feminine, is yours to give freely with no strings attached. As a spiritual discipline, it will free you.

After talking to Christine, I had an image of standing on a cliff in a long Goddess dress, stretching out my arms in front of me, feeling the wind against my back gently supporting me in sending love energy across the ocean to someone I wanted to control so that I would stay "happy". For many months I had tapped into my ego's need for security of my emotional state and the vulnerability of an open heart was not an option. When I experienced the visualization and entered into my sacred heart that wants and needs nothing, my energy switched entirely from "me" to "we"—not just the "we" of my relationship, but the "we" of humanity. When I visualize sending love and feeling it, the act extends to all people and all of Life.

The power of focusing on moment-by-moment radical love in service to another is that it dissolves the "I" of the ego. The Divine Feminine does not exist as "I"; it is unity and connection and togetherness; it is about bringing people to a common bond to experience the touch of God through each other and the tenderness of nature. It is interesting to note the word "serve" and "deserve". When I am fearful, I immediately think of what I deserve to have in my life or how I may not deserve something based on feelings of unworthiness. Either way, the focus is entirely on my ego self. But when I serve, the focus becomes "we"—everyone benefits from the service of radical love as it transcends from the individual to the shared experience. I cannot serve another without filling myself with love. This is a great spiritual law and one that will bring you continual peace if you practice it.

Another simple and profound way to bring yourself from heartache to heart-full states is to breathe gratitude into your body for all the amazing lessons and gifts and cherished memories. Even though you may feel rejected or betrayed or isolated due to the actions or words of your partner, remember that your partner or past love is here to help strengthen your capacity to love. I have no doubt that our souls are here in present time to grow in love; an intimate relationship is an opportunity to do that and is a gift regardless of the outcome.

In marriage, my husband and I triggered each other's insecurities and unhelpful beliefs for years. When I began to breathe through my feelings, releasing them and allowing space for gratitude to come in, I experienced an acceptance and willingness to apologize, forgive and be compassionate much more quickly. At first it would take me a week to get over what I experienced as an unkind remark, then a few days and finally it would be less than an hour. Each time that I practiced breathing in gratitude, I reminded myself that he is a mirror showing me my core beliefs about who I am and what I am. Because of him, I had a chance to choose again, to see the lies that built my identity and bring forth the light and love and power of my spirit.

As you grow in consciousness, your ego mind will fight to bring you back into neediness and drama. As much as I practiced gratitude and reminding myself of the gifts in my rocky relationship, there were still times when I chose to be a victim, stumbling over my own "story". The more I tried to be "enlightened" and be true to my spiritual values, the more demanding, pushy and whiny my inner voices became. Inevitably, this culminated in me arguing with my husband or experiencing suppressed anger that exploded with wild abandon at a moment's notice. Since then, I've learned that every once in awhile, I just need to flow with the person that presents herself in my body, if simply to observe her and acknowledge that she has been heard.

Remember that you are the observer and that you can choose to change the movie playing on your screen at any time. You are one with the screen, but you are *not* the movie itself. I recognized that my ego self was part of the movie I played out and that she would return on occasion to perform in sequels to the original screenplay. Eventually, her star role would become a minor part, as I learned to accept her and be gentle with her.

On occasion, I find it useful to cut the chords of fear—the energetic ties between myself and a loved one that may interfere with allowing us to be completely free. In this case, I ask Archangel Michael, who is often envisioned with sword in hand, to cut the chords and allow these fear-based attachments to be transmuted back to love energy. If you do this, your partner may sense or think of you as these chords are cut, but know that it is a loving act that is gentle for all involved. (You will intuitively sense when it is done, or you can ask Source to help you hear or see the completion of it.) This loving act also helps you to come back to the present moment and be aware of when you may be creating new chords of fear that attach themselves to people you think you need or people you have not forgiven.

If you want to attract someone into your life, first ask yourself, "Am I in service to Life or do I need something out of Life right now? This is a question to thoroughly contemplate. The strongest relationship you will ever have in your life will come not because you found "the one", but because of your spiritual maturity in the principles of self-trust, divine trust, surrender, compassion and forgiveness. The more you master these principles, the less needy you become. Regardless of the nature of your relationship, it cannot thrive with neediness at the forefront. Admitting that you are needy and investing time and effort in these principles will prepare you for when you do meet your heart-mate. As Marianne Williamson says, we can all attract our ideal partner, the question is whether we can keep that relationship once it arrives.

With Marianne's wisdom, another question I invite you to ask yourself is: "Am I the partner that my heart-mate is ready to meet, or would I feel the need to control my partner with expectations, assumptions and beliefs?" If you are still feeling needy (and even when you're not) go back to your spiritual practice and trust that the timing of meeting someone may not be at that very moment. Release emotion, accept and love your thoughts and center into a peaceful meditation where you fill your own body with love and then vibrate that love into the world.

Now you may be ready to feel this loving service more and more throughout the day. As you encounter different people and situations, be aware of cultivating a moment-by-moment presence of heart, opening in love and compassion to each person and each situation. You do not have to use your intellect to always know what to say or do; you can simply breathe through your heart and send love in service to that person, situation, or environment. This energy of being the love that you are attracts a beloved and soothes troubled relationships. It is the presence of now, the heart of the Virgin.

MEDITATIVE REFLECTIONS
FOR THE VIRGIN HEART

♥ Each moment, here in my body, I begin again.

♥ You can find me everywhere. Now.

♥ I am the miracle; you are the gift.

Presence and the Virgin Heart

3

THE MOTHER HEART: GUILT, ACCEPTANCE AND RADICAL LOVE

THE MOTHER HEART LOVES and accepts us unconditionally. Hers is a radical love where everything that you are, everything that you feel and everything that you have ever thought or acted on, is embraced in warm light. It is the Heart within each of us that knows no judgment, has no expectations and opens to all of Life as love. It is also the Heart that women have difficulty embodying, mostly due to lies they were told as young girls. These lies stick to women's thought patterns and become Velcro Voices that are designed to punish, belittle, or stop transformation. They attempt to block the portal of the Mother Heart, which naturally gives and receives love as an expression of Life. They are the voices of suffering and the keepers of guilt.

Do you believe the voice within that talks to you and at you? Most people do. They think it proves the very existence of their roles and identity formed throughout life: mother, friend, wife, partner, colleague, daughter, sister. They allow the voice to defend or defeat the personalities within each of these identities: the Mother Bear, the Loyal Friend, the Nurturing Wife, the Passionate Partner, the Dedicated Colleague, the Unworthy Daughter, the Misfit Sister. Whatever the thoughts, whether you view them as good or bad, they stick to your identity—if you choose to believe them. Your choice determines the extent to which you suffer and feel guilt, the lowest energetic vibration on the planet.

I am certain that few people go about wondering if Mary experienced guilt in her lifetime. After all, they would reason, she likely did not hurt anyone and never made bad decisions. While we will never know for sure the workings of Mary's mind, she did have a life that was filled with opportunity to suffer and feel guilt within that suffering. Because guilt is a way of resisting what is, of not loving what is at this moment, she could have destroyed herself by not accepting fact: that she was pregnant out of wedlock, that she had to flee her home for her safety and the safety of her family; that she was told her baby would become a man who would experience extreme suffering and rejection; that she witnessed the prophecy come true; that she witnessed her community support the killing of her son.

Place yourselves for one moment in this woman's situation and imagine what sorrow and suffering would keep your body in dis-ease, to make you want to give up on life. Imagine the guilt of, "What if I could have acted differently, done something else to change this outcome?" That is what the vast majority of us do when we are in a place of suffering, regardless of whether it is logical or not. If this form of questioning is a result of our Velcro thoughts, the suffering intensifies and keeps us there. Part of Mary's Code, then, is being free of the Velcro thoughts. I have no doubt these thoughts came through her at times as they did when Christ, about to die on the cross asks, "My God my God why have you forsaken me?" But then, just as Christ immediately accepts the situation and his life's greater purpose, so too does Mary allow thoughts to leave her mind. Because the thought does not define her, she can better learn to trust in the Divine.

In Cheri Huber's book, *Making a Change For Good: A Guide to Compassionate Self-Discipline*, I completed a thirty-day program which trains people to disidentify with thoughts. Huber says that the thought itself does not have any energy of its own—we give it energy by either participating in it or resisting it—often using the same tactics for both (examples: storytelling, meaning-making). Velcro Voices trigger lengthy dialogues in our minds that take us out of the present moment and into the past or future; they encourage us to feel anger, sadness, jealousy, rage, injustice and a host of other unhelpful states. The thoughts themselves might even appear to be helpful by convincing us that we are right and another person just isn't as spiritually evolved (poor thing). This is a subtle form of separation too, as it becomes an easy way of believing we are special and others are not. Eventually, this type of thinking leads us back to guilt as we judge ourselves for not being as evolved as we thought we were.

You can choose not to believe a thought, regardless of how right or reasonable it appears to be. Breathe through the thought, feel it and choose to witness its departure. There will you begin to taste the freedom of living in the Divine Feminine; living in the radical heart of love.

JOURNAL INSIGHTS:
STANDING OUTSIDE THE TRIBE

I am beginning to believe that I am not "cut out" for marriage. Why can't I just be happy, for God's sake? There must be a key ingredient missing from my personality or basic constitution that if I could just find that, then all would be well. I could go back to entering the tribe, my family. Every time I see children with both their mother and father, I weep inside; that was my life. That is, until part of me shifted... where did I go? Why did I go? Is that part of me waiting out in space somewhere, wanting desperately to return?

These questions led me to guilt that was wrapped up in my identity. When I realized I was no longer who I thought I was and so did not have a quick and easy answer to replace the old identity, the "me" in transition was led to guilt. Ego does not like change and, in particular, attacks the space of transition where life is uncertain. My thought that there was something inherently wrong with me for leaving my husband became all-pervasive during this transition. I was no longer a "wife", no longer "Mrs." I didn't know how to refer to myself when filling out forms or when referring to my husband—not my ex and not my husband...what do I call him? The guilt of not being able to name him or my relationship to him was steeped in identity loss. Who am I when I can no longer simply define my most primary relationship of the last fifteen years?

Looking back at the suffering, I see that I was associating my identity with loss; I was resisting fact, (that I initiated our separation) and indulging in meaning-making (I am destroying our relationship, our lives and my children's lives). Fact became a story laden with guilt; a story that proved I was unworthy and flawed—a basic lie that many of us begin to believe at a very young age. At times of great uncertainty, it seems that the void, the space where we can sink into the mystery of not knowing who we are, where we are going, or how our future will unfold, is the greatest gift to our spirit and the greatest curse to our ego mind. The mind wants to fill the void with certainty, to prove our unhelpful beliefs about self and, in so doing, overshadow the feminine flow of simply loving what is and trusting that all is well.

SACRED PRACTICE

♥ *If you are in a transition or you sense that one is arriving, begin the spiritual practice of feeling the empty space within and the mind that wants to control it. Sense the sorrow, suffering and guilt that take their space in this holy land. Breathe into all of it and feel it fully. It does not need a permanent residence; it just needs an outlet to be released. Go deep into the heart of your feeling; breathe deeply and with intensity through your pain and stay with this feeling and stay in your body. When you feel complete, consciously release the Velcro Voices. Give them up (they will return at some point and constant acceptance with release is required).*

♥ *As you release, be aware that you are not ignoring the voices or suppressing them, but you are choosing not to believe them. This is a distinction that will help you to embrace your feminine heart, because the Feminine is the love of what is; by resisting the voices, labeling them as bad, or pretending they don't exist, you risk closure of your Sacred Heart.*

With the love of what is, your thoughts are unable to separate you from your divine nature. Bring your body into this truth. If you wish, you can do this by asking Mary's love to be felt in your body; ask to feel the love that you are—her love and your essence are One. It is this feeling that anchors you and grounds you in the place of peace as you feel the war within subsiding.

♥ *If you notice your mind wants to continue reading but your heart is telling you to stop and do the exercise above, release your resistance and excuses and enter into the experience of being with both the illusion of your pain and the truth of love. In my own spiritual practice, there is nothing as powerful as engaging in these opposites. It is as though my soul wants me to see just how different truth and illusion are by placing them up against each other—first observing the mind, then feeling into the body and last, being with and in Spirit.*

As young girls, many of us were aware of what a "bad" girl and a "good" girl looked like, acted like and thought like. We believed what our parents, institutions and culture taught us about bad and good behavior in little girls, teens and adult women. We either accepted the role of the Good Girl and tried hard to conform in order to be accepted, or we resisted and became the Bad Girl who rebelled to prove her worth outside her tribe. Either way, guilt is a conditioned response from the collective mind of "the group". This mind's function is to point out every wrongdoing and replays these as stories to slot you into the label of good girl/bad girl. Unfortunately, many women experienced this as part of their religion, schooling or work, and are still dealing with the destructive belief systems that formed.

I find it fascinating that many of us have similar stories about how the good girl and bad girl identities shaped our lives and the guilt we live with. Being the youngest and only girl, I wanted to fit in with my brother's friends and realized that becoming a boy was the best way to do that. Experience also taught me that being a boy meant that I was less likely to be hurt, rejected, or shamed. I was praised by my father for having male qualities and noticed that I received more attention when I acted like a boy. At the same time, I formed stories about girls and their unpredictable behavior and crying—being a boy satisfied my reasoning mind. I began to shape the idea that a good girl was in reality a boy, and that a bad girl tried to be even more of a girl and use her "girlness" to manipulate others.

Sacred Practice

In your own journey into feelings of guilt, ask yourself how much of your guilt stems from beliefs that are part of your Good Girl/Bad Girl identity. In fact, list all of your perceptions of good girl and then do the same for bad girl; write down how good girls think, act and behave. Do the same for bad girls. Then go through your list and see what violations your conditioned mind believes you have committed and to what extent you are still carrying the weight of this violation. Inquire into why you have not released this guilt or why you feel guilty when a similar situation arises and triggers the Velcro Voices. Begin to keep track of these unhelpful voices associated to being bad or good and if these voices have a particular personality. Note who, if anyone, the voice reminds you of and how many of them appear to be authority figures that come from patriarchal institutions (school, religion, government, family). By observing your voices and inquiring into them, the guilt keeps a healthy distance, unable to attach itself to your identity.

OPENING TO YOUR GUILT, FEAR AND DARKNESS

In bringing myself to the Mother Heart, I had to learn that it was okay to fully feel all the unwanted emotions and thoughts that ran through my body and mind. I had to come to a level of trust of both myself and the Divine Mother. This trust was about knowing I would be accepted and loved within my full expression of anger, within my least loving thoughts. I had lived many years without this trust and found that when I ignored and suppressed what I judged as unloving or weak, I could not tell the truth to anyone, including myself, loved ones, or God. Because my heart was clouded, my intuitive nature closed down and I entered a period of numbness, which I interpreted as a healing. I believed that lack of emotion meant that I was learning to cope with loss; I learned well the patriarchal value of keeping my chin up and going through life with a "positive attitude". Deep down, the anger and sadness lurked, waiting to be released. As Carl Jung says, what isn't released, what is not consciously brought to the forefront, eventually reveals itself as fate.

Here is a poem about my unwanted, fear-based energies and what happens when I choose not to accept them:

SLEEPING GIANT

Keep away from me
I am dark
evil
make bad things happen
I can't be trusted
(even as you read this
doubt fills your head)
maybe this IS the truth
maybe I am all of that
and more
I depend on your belief
trust that you will find your way
to goodness and light
from dark corridors
the shadow of my heart
never touched
discovered
uncovered
it sees silently
goes quietly
to its cave
a sleeping giant
buried
in goodbye.

I believe two pivotal moments helped me to open to all emotions. The first was reading David Deida's book, *Blue Truth*, and knowing that I can open as any strong emotion and be the love that I am; be one with God. Society teaches us that emotion is our true identity: she is a bad girl because she has temper tantrums; he is a lost soul because he mopes around all day. Yet opening to emotion gave me great freedom to communicate my whole being. I started to feel the essence of this stranger and have gratitude for both its arrival and for the process of saying goodbye to it, reflecting on the lessons it taught me. Now, each time it arrives, I am aware of the opportunity to remain in my essence instead of turning away. Jesus was an example of someone who displayed anger publically on a number of occasions while staying true to his higher self. For most people, meaning-making, assumptions, beliefs and judgments get in the way of Virgin emotion; but knowing this pure emotion is possible makes me much more conscious of when and how my conditioned mind starts to taint this purity.

Another support in assisting me to open to unwanted feeling is breath work. Some people refer to it as rebirthing or transformational breath; it is a way of breathing that stirs emotions that are part of the body's memory but not necessarily accessible to our conscious mind. When the emotions are then felt fully and released with the help of a trained facilitator, there is the opportunity to bring all parts back to the unity of the heart.

JOURNAL INSIGHTS: RESISTANCE TO THE ROLE

As I write this book, I notice my passion for the purity of radical love; yet as I enter deep into the heart of the Mother, I am surprised at my resistance around the word "mother" and the conditioned Velcro Voices that refuse to accept and love the mother within me.

Prior to being a mother, I found myself shaking my head at the things mothers said or did when with their children. It seemed to me that they were the least conscious beings on the planet. And then I became one. The struggle to be the perfect, loving, nurturing, patient role model for my children turned into a deep, bitter self-rejection. Shortly after my son was born he cried relentlessly every day for a year, with a brief reprieve from midnight until five a.m. The doctors said, "Just rock him to sleep." I said, "He doesn't like to be rocked," to which a very young nurse proclaimed my ignorance, "That's impossible. All children like to be rocked." I went home with my crying baby in my arms and plunged myself into feelings of worthlessness for a lifetime role I would never be fit for.

IDENTITY, ROLES AND THE HEART OF THE MOTHER

I began to separate myself from every literal and symbolic mother on the planet; even my love for Mother Nature and my spiritual connection to Mary waned with my fear of being labeled a Fraud Mother. The guilt tormented me for many years, until I was presented with a miracle.

When my oldest son Matthew turned eight, we took a family trip to beautiful Lake Okanagan and my trapped mother identity was broken open. I had created in my mind the perfect family vacation and looked forward to being together peacefully and creating new adventures. On the first day of our trip I was thrown into "reality": I was once again furious due to yet another argument with Matthew whom I perceived as being belligerent and defiant. I felt I would never get through to him. The next morning, when everyone was still asleep, I tiptoed out of the hotel room and down to the water's edge. I asked God, "What do I do? I have tried the advice of all the parenting books that are supposedly the good ones. I've listened to and tested the advice of my friends, and still nothing. What do I do with this child?" I demanded, throwing my arms up to the heavens. What happened next was the beginning of my journey into the heart. A soft, gentle voice within replied, "Love him. Love him fully, love him completely, love him." I dropped to my knees in the sand and cried for a very long time with this miracle message resonating in my heart.

It was in this truth that all the judgments about myself began to dissolve. The more I stayed in the present moment of love with my children the more I came to know that this was real—the rest was the story of my life. Now, four years later, I share a closeness with Matthew and my younger son Mitchell that fills me with gratitude and joy; we daily express our love for each other. I hear the peace of "I love you" that echoes from their smiles and lips as they go about their day.

This truth also came through my experience as a daughter. Three days before my father's sudden death, I called to see how he was doing, and he whispered the words he had never expressed to me during our earth-time together, "I love you." I believe my father's diagnosis of liver cancer led to him opening his heart. This is the

Mother energy in all of us, the deepest will to express our love for one another. When that natural energy is suppressed, as it was for me the first eight years of mothering, the wisdom of the feminine heart is muffled and all forms of intuition and relationship connections begin to deteriorate too. Closure of the heart equals a managed life. Only heart opening can lead to a magnified life where there is joy, wild abandon, curiosity, freedom, awe and vitality.

THE GOOD DAUGHTER BREAKS DOWN

When doing breath work with Master Rebirther, Mahara Brenna, I recognized that I still held at bay my own mother and myself as a mother—they were nowhere near my heart because of the grave disappointment at my failure as a mother and daughter. I convinced myself that I didn't deserve to be a mother nor could I even measure up to the nurturing daughters around me who took care of their mothers. I wasn't the motherly or daughterly "type" (whatever that is, remains a mystery to me).

After completing the healing breathing session, bringing mother and daughter together in my heart, I knew I had to release the image and roles of Mother and Daughter. I realized that for most of my life, they were connected to a contract created in my conditioned mind, where both of us needed to behave in a particular way to be considered worthy. I created a role that was so far removed from what gave me life and joy, that even if I could fulfill the role, I would be miserable doing it. For example, I know that my mother loves to shop and malls make me nervous; she loves her TV programs and I love to read and write; she loves to keep tidy and organized and I would rather use my time to create. Somewhere in this contrast I thought I needed to be like her in order to be worthy of being a daughter.

Every time she complained about her life I believed I needed to fit into her ideal daughter role I fabricated to support my belief. I denied what made my heart sing, ignoring my path and purpose each time I felt her negative emotion. Eventually, I became so angry with myself for rejecting my own needs that I withdrew almost completely from our relationship, deciding that no one could *make* her happy.

It took many months of this before I settled into looking within rather than pointing the finger at her. I saw my lack of self-forgiveness at closing my heart to the woman who gave birth to me and cared for me in the only way she knew how. I saw the great leap of faith she made to live with me after my father died and how the conditioned part of me took on responsibility for filling the loss she was experiencing.

My own loss was deep and heavy and I felt the burden of replacing my father. Five years after his passing I began to resurrect self-hatred for not being able to fill the space of loss and be the Good Daughter. My saving grace was my spiritual practice of stopping and taking time out to love myself, not as a role (mother/daughter) or as an identity (good girl/good mother), but in the space of shared Mary energy—the inner feeling and knowing that I am one with Divine Love.

As I went back and forth between spiritual self mothering and submersion in Velcro Voices, I discovered that this healing also involved my fears about being an orphan; I had already lost my father and I was not about to lose my mother. I wanted to be fully accepted by my mother and felt that would be impossible to do if I lived a big and glorious version of myself, parading in front of her that I was "getting on with my life". So when we were together I would play small and talk negative and be depressed to match what I thought was her inner state while she grieved my father's passing. At first I thought I was doing this for her benefit, to keep her from further despair, but much later realized it was more about my own need to be accepted and loved. I had succumbed to a common belief that clouds the heart of wisdom: If I keep myself wounded, I will be loved. In the moment of this realization, I began to heal from our relationship pattern and simultaneously come back to the heart of Mother love.

In deep meditation, Mary revealed that in order to love ourselves fully, the relationship to Mother must be healed. It is by opening to Mother energy that the world experiences unity and profound healing. It is in the rejection of Mother (all forms of "mother") that we remain separate, disconnected and apathetic. We are mother to the All; we are mother to each other; we are mother to the earth. Mary is calling the Sacred Feminine within women and men to become actively involved in the mothering of Life. The intense level of passion and devotion and compassion often seen in mothers of newborns is the same degree to which we are being called to mother others, animals, our blessed earth. It is the infinite and outrageous love that will bring us back home to ourselves, each other and the world.

CONTROL AND THE MOTHER HEART

Whether you have children or not, every woman has the mother aspect—that of radical love that nurtures, is compassionate and gives freely, opening to Life itself. When the Mother Heart is blocked by fear of loss, fear of chaos, fear of unhappiness and suffering, it begins to close and eventually shut down.

As the Mother Heart shuts down, the Shadow Mother emerges, with thoughts and actions that control and limit self, other people, the environment and the Universe. The Shadow Mother leaves her heart and flees to the perceived safety of the conditioned mind that tells her to act in ways that will limit suffering.

While writing part of this book from Ashland, Oregon, I sat next to a family in a café and overheard the conversation of a mother and father, arguing over the eating patterns of their child. Grandmother was there, quietly eating her soup while the mother ranted on for the entire meal about how the child ought to have regular eating times and how inconsiderate her partner was for even thinking of not stopping for regular eating time, and why did he feel the need to cater to *his* mother, who surely could wait for their arrival. After all, *she* is the grown up, not the child…and on it went. At the end of the meal, the mother was extremely agitated and no doubt miserable for the remainder of the trip. Why? I believe she allowed her conditioned mind to take over without listening to her Mother Heart that is the mother not only of her child but to everyone and everything around her. The Mother Heart had shut down while the controlling conditioned mind took over.

We have all heard and been part of experiences like this; women intuitively know that the voice of the conditioned mind never aligns with the voice of the Mother Heart and they feel the disconnect in anger, depression, or confusion. In this disconnect, they hear the call of their Mother Heart, but are trained through schooling and societal expectations to follow the mind that tries desperately to warn them of the dangers of following the heart. After all, there is nothing more unreasonable to the conditioned mind than radical love—the full complete, need nothing, no conditions love. Boundless, radical love is our essence. And yet...

I have struggled long and hard with control issues. I am aware of why they are there and recognize their voices. When I started to hear the voices and not believe them they came back, more adamant in their agenda to show me that control over every moment of the day would be the only thing that would save me. The louder they spoke the more I recognized that I could choose to leave my Mother Heart or choose not to believe the voices. It wasn't that I tried to send the voices away or become angry with them. I simply chose not to believe them anymore.

If you listen carefully to your voices of control you may find that they are adult-sounding, like an authority figure who is the expert. After repeated listening to the messages and nuances of the voice, you may discover it represents an authority figure from your past, perhaps a parent, perhaps a teacher; you developed the habit of internalizing their direction. But the direction was for the child you were not the adult you are. The direction is outdated and needs to be put to rest. I have found two ways to approach the relentless voice; one is to not believe it. The other is to acknowledge it and accept that it is there, rather than pretending it's not there or angrily sending it away.

If you do choose to inquire about the appearance of the voice, my friend and business coach, Mary Ellen Sanajko, suggests asking, "What do you need from me right now?" When I ask this question, I inevitably get the answer that is driving it. Usually it has something to do with trying to protect me from change. It may be something entirely different for you yet asking the question often lessens the tyrant quality of the voice.

CONTROL AND SELFISHNESS: A NEW PERSPECTIVE

In all the motherhood images in the media, selflessness is still a primary assumption. Women are supposed to give tirelessly of themselves. It is in this cultural molding that they begin to hear the voice of judgment that causes them to feel less-than, to fear they will never measure up. This fear is actually what stimulates selfishness. I believe that selfishness is not so much being absorbed in our wants and needs as it is the constant fear of lack, the fear of loss, the fear of love's absence.

When someone close to me would tell me that I was selfish, I either reacted by resisting their claims or I escaped the conversation so that they could not see my steady stream of tears. I labeled myself a bad mother and wife because I chose to believe their accusations. What I could not see is that selfishness is not who I am; it is not my identity. I desperately needed guidance that would help me to see it for what it was at that time in my life: the fear of failure, of not being successful. This fear drove me to be so future-oriented that I could not be in the present. I was convinced that stopping in present time would jeopardize my chance at achieving my goals. I accepted the identity of "selfish" and resisted it at the same time, unsure of how to "fix" myself.

Now I help women entrepreneurs redefine words like selfish and balance. I ask them to write down their definition of these words and then to see how much of the definition comes from media, family and cultural influences. Inevitably, they discover that their conditioned mind has held them hostage to narrow definitions which limit their freedom and happiness. I ask them to feel selfishness in the body and to feel balance in the body; this goes beyond the intellectual mind to the experience of the Divine Feminine. I ask them to consider what balance would look like if they allowed their fears of lack and loss and unworthiness (the cause of selfishness) to be released.

With intimate relationships, selfishness is again, not what it may seem on the surface. I recently was humbled to see how my deep fears of losing someone ignited old habits of selfishness. I found myself not wanting to hear his thoughts, his concerns, his joys, for fear of feeling that I wasn't enough in the relationship, which would lead to loss. I did not want my identity as a "good catch" to be shattered! After trying yet again to control a phone conversation, I felt the urge to go within and nurture my Mother Heart, connecting with Mary. I heard her say, "Feel into him." This guidance, in Mary's typical style, was short yet profound, and I knew intuitively that I was to travel the path of unity, the path of the Divine Feminine. On this path, selfishness does not exist because I am not attached to the "me" that is wanting to keep safe and unchanged; I am not invested in the "I" who has a particular identity. I am not separate from another. My guidance was to open completely to experiencing directly what this man was experiencing without the filter and separation of "I". My guidance was to feel into all of his experience without meaning-making that initiates my anxiety or sense of the "happy" self. The next morning I called him and excitedly explained my breakthrough understanding. I felt my whole life was a race away from intimacy and at last I understood the true freedom of the Divine Feminine—unity with another.

THE TRICKY VOICE OF PARTIAL CONTROL

Once I was aware of the voices of control, I developed an awareness of my more subtle tendencies to control. These tendencies were accompanied by voices that also stopped my personal will from surrendering to Divine Will. Voices of partial control appear benign because they have a spiritual, loving flavor. They are designed to be the loving voices of reason, telling you why things are not going in your favor and why you are in the midst of challenge or chaos. They gently remind you to be loving and compassionate and create reasons for the behavior of other people that may hurt you. But because you are conscious, you tell yourself, he is an angry person and it has nothing to do with me, or she is jealous and that is why she attempts to betray me. In giving these reasonable answers to your reasoning mind, you are trying to insulate yourself from suffering. While it is a stage of consciousness that is needed and helps many people to perceive a situation in a more helpful manner, it still does not require a deeper level of spiritual maturity.

Deeper maturity accepts people and situations exactly as they are without the need to control them through the reasoning mind. We use this subtle control in order not to suffer. I know this through experience; my sense is that each ego has its ways of introducing control in such a way that the evolved self accepts it as a higher truth.

What would happen if instead of making assumptions about an undesired event or act we really felt the loss, felt the rejection, cleared our Mother Heart of this veil of emotion, opened Her to the situation and people involved with a pure, radical heart? If we are afraid to feel, the need to control will always arise.

Another subtle form of control is attitude toward time. I notice that when I am in meditation and not in the present moment I often hear the voice of Time that says, "Waste of time; not enough time in the day; look at your massive to-do list." Again, these voices seem reasonable because they appear to be what I need if I am to achieve and accomplish goals. Yet these voices cause my body to feel off, and I am reminded of the disconnect between my Mother Heart and my conditioned mind.

Perhaps you might relate to the voice of time and how it can control and begin to shut down the Mother Heart. In Malcolm Gladwell's book, *Blink*, he discusses a case study where people in a rush to get somewhere did not stop to help someone who was in obvious need of medical assistance (planted for the study). It was determined that the vast majority of people, regardless of their financial status, education, or spiritual path, are conditioned to close their hearts when they perceive a lack of time to fulfill their plans.

For the Mother Heart time is not linear and does not exist with the meaning that our patriarchal society gives it. It is the being-ness that sits with the moon and bathes in the sun, receiving love and then giving it out in glorious measure. This sense of being, this feminine aspect of God, was not one I was accustomed to and it was met with great resistance when I began my practice of meditating. My whole life, "sitting" was not acceptable and relaxing was not in my vocabulary. The voice of Time was only satisfied if I was producing a tangible product. I remember my friend Kristy asking me once while I was in a frenzy, "What do you do to relax?" When I told her, "nothing" she was astounded. I thought it was quite normal, having known nothing else. Yet I was aware of my adrenal glands working hard to keep me in overdrive—I just didn't know that in my extreme doing, I was scared to death of being. I had given myself over to my mind to control every aspect of my life and my relationships suffered because of it.

When my oldest son was three, I remember him grabbing my leg and crying, and I looked down, shocked that he was upset. I asked, "What's wrong honey?" and he said, "Mommy, you never listen to me anymore." He had been trying to tell me something and I, wrapped up in thoughts of the future and past, did not even hear him. I was not "here". My beliefs about time and using every minute of it, invaded my relationships and I could only see this through the eyes of my baby. At first, I went into shame over my selfishness with wanting to accomplish and achieve at the expense of my family. Much later, I saw my selfishness for what it really was: my fear of lack of time and my inability to control that lack.

When people think of the controlling mother they often think of mother's wish to keep her babies safe—it is what is shown in dramatic movies and in grocery stores when little Johnny is scolded for running into another aisle. Yet the more subtle control, that of keeping safe by living in the future and past, is much more common. This requires great awareness for mothers as they can easily misinterpret the instinct of keeping loved ones safe with the conditioned mind whose job goes far beyond physical safety; it actually believes that no change is best for everyone in the family.

In a medical intuition on-line course I heard Dr. Norman Shealey say the reason people don't stay in present time is because they don't believe in themselves. This statement felt like a heavy weight in my body. I was humbled once again in witnessing how I was showing up again in my relationship to time: my kids were out of school for summer holidays and I needed to complete the writing of this book; my thoughts were consumed with the lack of time available to do just that, and I spent my "Be Here Now" time with my kids in Never Never Land (never never going to finish the book land). As my thoughts concentrated on lack of time, I began to doubt my ability to not only complete the book, but to complete it well.

Suddenly I was hyper-aware of standards and deadlines. The ego identity of Author raised its head and preached to me that real authors would be committing more time and more care to their books than I was. I recognized the authority figure in this voice. Student and expert were suddenly at odds with one another and neither one of them were prepared to give up.

CONTROL AND THE SUBPERSONALITY

Through my Author Voice experience, I discovered that each voice has a personality of its own, and the challenge is to distance self from these subpersonalities and see them for what they are—the effect of experiences in which I chose to believe things about myself and others. These choices, usually made at a very young age, form beliefs constantly reinforced by the non-supportive authority figure who continues to live on in the mind long after childhood. These voices become part of the habitual "mind crap" and take on a distinct personality of a certain type of authority figure— sometimes it may even be a single person, but often the voices are a composite of authority figures.

It is helpful to write down the subpersonality, its characteristics and the language it uses, so that you clearly see the voice is not you. As this is consistently recorded, there will be less reaction and resistance. Over time you will no longer believe it. As an example, I describe my Authority figure as the author who knows more than I do. He is much better organized and tends to be arrogant about his work (yes the subpersonality can be a different gender). My Student is the one who resists the Author and stubbornly refuses to do any work, or if work is done, she is not energized by it, but rather depressed because she knows she will be judged, and judged harshly. Neither one of these subpersonalities is Me. Byron Katie, author of *Loving What Is: Four Questions That Can Change Your Life*, is known as a truly enlightened person, yet even she experiences those voices...she just chooses not to believe them.

It is also helpful to remind yourself that the mind is a tool—nothing more, nothing less. However, in *The End of Your World*, author Adyashanti says this is one of our greatest challenges: "The mind is not seen as a tool, but instead, as the source of a sense of self. Most people are constantly asking their mind, 'Who am I?' 'What is life?' 'What is true?' They're looking to their mind to tell them what should and shouldn't be. This is ridiculous! You wouldn't go into your garage and ask your hammer who you are or what's the right or wrong thing to do."

Medical intuitive and author, Caroline Myss, says the mind is nothing more than a fact archive. Although it is not meant to take on the definition of who you are this is most often the case. For example, your co-worker tells you that you forgot to fax an important document. You know this is fact and your fact archive records it. Then you allow the fact archive to argue with its own reality. It allows a subpersonality to do this: the Authority figure begins to judge the fact that you forgot. It judges your lack of responsibility. Then you allow the fact archive to enter with another subpersonality: the Victim: It says you were under a time crunch and judges your boss for giving you too many things to do each day. It judges your co-worker for pointing out the fact that you forgot. And it gives you free reign to be miserable for the rest of the day.

When you experience these personalities on a conscious level you begin to awaken to the truth that everything you believe about the world and about yourself have been given over to the conditioned mind—an understanding we have on an intellectual level. But for many women, when we feel emotion, the personalities, the voices; everything seems so real and it is difficult to rise above it.

For years I stuffed my emotions and pretended they did not exist. I didn't get PMS and did not understand "all that crying". When I neared my forties and was struggling with all my close relationships I began to rediscover all the sadness and anger that I kept hidden for so long. This discovery was wonderful because it allowed me to clear the debris around my heart and live from my whole body. It felt good. Unfortunately, I began to make "meaning" of it. If I was angry, I started to label myself as someone who was in need of massive healing; someone who would take years to get back on her feet again. If I was sad, I would define myself as depressed, uncertain and needy. It felt "good" to believe it. After all, I didn't have to change anything and could relax in my childlike innocence. That is, of course, until the Authority subpersonality took over and told me to "Get A Life!"

I felt trapped in a cycle of feel-good and not-feel-good. Slowly, there was an awareness that contemplation would help dissolve the cycle; to inquire about the emotion rather than make it mean something or allow it to define me. Inquiry is not meaning-making that attaches itself to who we are. It is the process of discovering what we are not to return to who we are. Good questions to ask are: What is this emotion trying to tell me? Does it have a belief attached to it? These questions help create non-attachment to the emotion and help in seeing it as part of human experience, rather than the essence of who we are.

𝔍OURNAL 𝔍NSIGHTS: 𝔗HE 𝔒BSERVER

This morning I feel sad and wishing and hoping for love, connection, touch. I am feeling it and am aware that as I begin to cry I am watching myself; I am the observer seeing a familiar pattern. I see it with compassion and allow it to unfold to release the tears, the needy thoughts; I watch the drama unfold. "I need you." I notice the thought; I notice my feelings; and I don't become it nor do I resist it. I am a compassionate third party and it feels strange and oddly satisfying to have this sensation that she—the one who believes the Voice—is part of me, but not the me that is my core, my essence. I love her, but I no longer have to be her or be defined by her. I am not definable. I am free, even in this sadness.

When Mary gave birth to Jesus, I imagine that the separating, the illusion of separating from the Mother Heart, was healed. Through Mary, Jesus began to teach others to heal separation with the Mother. There is a touching story of Jesus that takes place shortly before his crucifixion. He takes a disciple's hand and puts it in Mary's and says, "This is your mother." And to her, "This is your son." The meaning of this gesture is to be with all humankind as a family, to love them as a family. I believe that Jesus had an additional Divine Feminine message: we all have a relationship, a direct connection with the Sacred Feminine. It is real and it is accessible while we are here on earth.

The healing of the relationship with Mother leads to caring for the environment, walking softly and gently with Her beneath our feet supporting us; breathing Her in the air, feeling Her surround us. Her in the sunshine on our skin nurturing and cradling us in loving arms. The heart of the Mother lives here now. Bring it home to you, to us, to the All.

MEDITATIVE REFLECTIONS FOR THE MOTHER HEART

♥ I mother all of Life and Life mothers me.

♥ I observe the illusion with gentleness and compassion.

♥ I hear the Velcro Voice and can choose whether or not to believe it.

4

THE MOTHER HEART: SURRENDER AND FORGIVENESS

JOURNAL INSIGHTS: THE OTHER WOMAN

I am humbled through initiation into the world of single mom. I discover spreadsheets and financial statements, build biceps doing the masculine tasks I once took for granted and feel the emptiness of my house and body during my children's weekends with Dad. Despite the newness of much of my life, I think, "I can do this!" and proudly gain confidence that I will survive this new stage in my life. And then The Other Woman happened. Although separated for over a year, I did not entertain the possibility that my children would be eventually connecting with another woman. She showed up one day when my children were leaving on vacation with their dad. Smiling at me and telling me I live in a wonderful neighborhood, she zooms away with my children, who wave goodbye through tinted windows. My heart sinks as I realize that this stranger is filling the space of the seat I once sat in on family vacations. My mind begins to imagine: she is making small talk with my kids; she is taking them on adventures; she is working her way up to replace me...

Every woman who has experienced The Other Woman, regardless of the circumstances in which she arrives, knows this constriction of the heart. They know the full expansive emotion that comes with the shock of recognition: life will never be the same again. In this space, the need to control everyone and everything suddenly goes into high gear, or the opposite happens: a withdrawal from life, truth, love. I experienced both, depending on the hour and circumstance. While there is no one answer or path that nurtures our being as woman and Divine Feminine essence, I do believe in two secrets of the Mother Heart: surrender and forgiveness.

To me, surrender is opening my heart to all there is. It is an act of love; an act of unity that is the foundation of Sacred Feminine energy. The Mother Heart is radical because it is constantly surrendering in every moment. Mary is known to many as Mother not only because of her relationship with Jesus; she is Mother because of her complete willingness to surrender to the most horrific circumstances. As a mother, I was mortified by the existence of The Other Woman and surrender was the furthest thing from my mind. When I contemplate Mary's life, I am in awe at her ability to surrender to the weight of the unthinkable: the suffering and death of her child.

My friend Mary McTier recently lost her son Neil in a plane crash. When I first heard what happened, I could only think, "How will she survive this?" She was eighty-six and her husband ninety-six; and although she was in good health, I knew of many mothers who withered away with their child's passing. Over the next few months, I observed Mary carefully and came to marvel at her complete and utter surrender; at the miracle of her open heart; at the trust and faith in Spirit as she came to terms with Neil's death.

I asked Mary to share her experience of surrender. She told me that she would share with me on the condition that I make it clear that these ideas did not come from her, but from her loving guides, Archangel Michael and God. She said:

Surrender, to mankind, is a dirty word—you think you lose something—like property or rights. You are being robbed of something. With surrender and God, I have surrendered my will and life to God, but I do it in love, knowing that I'm receiving such pure unconditional love. I can only be blessed and lifted as a result of the surrender. And yet, it's not: "I'll surrender and then you comfort me and you'll be good to me." It's not a payback. True surrender is giving up ego and saying, "Ok God, I know I exist only because of your spirit giving me life, consciousness and awareness." When I die, the spirit within me doesn't die, it just goes on. So I'm not losing anything, I'm gaining everything. I'm surrendering not in order to gain, but because of love for God, Truth, Being.

I remember when both of my kids were in diapers. I cried and cried and said, "I surrender my child to you God. You've loaned him to me." In the human sense, I feel Neil belongs to me, yet he's not mine. He has to do his own separate trip. Most things in life we can find someone to lean on, but in this particular journey, we lean on, or surrender to God. So when Neil died, and I was asked to release him, that was surrendering him to God. I had to say, "Ok, he is yours and you loaned him to me for fifty-seven years, and he's gone to do his own thing, and I'm not going to be part of it." That's a surrender too; that I no longer have a say in his life. God gave me the wisdom to realize that it was important that I surrender and that it was the only thing I could do. It only causes pain to try to hold on to loved ones. Trust and have faith and know that by releasing and surrendering they go higher into other dimensions and they are doing what they need to do. I trust I will do what I need to do when my time comes. Surrender is a love and a trust; something in your spirit that you just know you need to do. It's for your own good. It is a joy and a blessing, and we can't go anywhere spiritually without surrendering, because if you are not surrendered, you are in ego and separation.

God does not force us to do anything. I understand Neil is on his own journey. We are all on our own journey. I surrender and let him be on his journey without me. Mothers always think we are part of our children's journey; I was told no, he (Neil) has to take his own journey, and we must know we're never alone.

After talking to my wise and dear friend, I saw how often I had resisted surrender to my children's divine path; to their journey that is separate from mine. I also saw how much strength and courage I had gained because of my constant opportunity to surrender, presented to me by virtue of being a mother. My dear friend Andrew Rezmer says that being a mother is synonymous with surrender, adding that from the moment of conception, mother experiences opportunity to love and release: "After the baby is born, their needs usually override mother's needs. She feeds them with her breast, with her unconditional love, with her fear, her values, her hopes. And when the children grow up, mother surrenders again as they go out into the world, and again when they find a partner who becomes the most important person in life, and mother gets the back seat or no seat at all. Mother's path is to give all, to give life starting from flesh and blood and to let it go eventually with no attachment or expectation."

Part of my personal difficulty in surrendering attachments to my family and others was my distrust in both the human and divine realm: I feared being alone on the earth journey. This showed up as fear of rejection and betrayal by those I was closest to. It showed up as a lack of trust in guidance, intimacy and connection. It shaped the control I could not let go of. Nowhere was this more apparent than when I entered the world of "single woman".

SURRENDER IN RELATIONSHIP

For most women, intimate relationships are a difficult aspect of surrender. For someone who is newly divorced, there is a vulnerability, a tenderness of the spirit that seeks from the outside, for touch, for proof that she is worthy of love and is loveable. For me, entering a loving relationship was a precarious venture: all was well until it wasn't.

I repeatedly took facts about my relationship and spun them into a story of why I was unhappy. As rage or sadness swept through my body, I felt even more of the "truth" of the story, as it gripped me in its claws. I had to do something to release myself and free both of us. I understood how reasonable surrender was; it made sense to my mind to "let go and let God." Until I tried it with my mind.

First I told myself to be in the moment; to be here now. Good advice and one that I repeat many times in this book. Yet the more I tried it, the louder the voices of resistance demanded that I have my way; that my expectations be met, especially the desired outcome. I wasn't ready to suddenly be in the now. I needed to look deeper into my need to control the outcome.

I inquired into where this need was coming from. Going right back to my early childhood I realized that my sensitivity to traumatic events had made my child's heart protect itself. I believe that one of the instinctual protections, even at that tender age, was to develop the belief that I alone am in control and that as long as I have full control I can prevent myself from being hurt. It also gave justification to hurt others who threaten to break through my wall of protection.

Armed with this new information, I thought that the awareness that I had come to would stop my misery. I thought I could handle the situation and conquer my fear. And yet each time I held a thought or image in my mind part of my body would react and the very outcomes I was trying to control began controlling me. I needed to go even deeper, to shed more layers and come back to the heart of truth.

I began to take apart my story and see where I was manipulating a fact and making it mean something based on beliefs I developed in my childhood. I looked at the beliefs I adopted: that there was something wrong with me, that I was flawed; that I was not worthy; that I could not speak my truth and be who I really was. Then I saw clearly how each part of the dramatic story of my relationship had an investment in one of those beliefs.

As my awareness of my patterns of thinking and behavior became clear, I thought that surrender could be mastered. Yet I continued to cry and found myself telling the same story over and over to all my friends who would listen. Although I now was equipped to make more reasonable choices and to change my thoughts, I found there was a part of me inside that refused to do that for good. I could manage to feel at peace for some days or hours or minutes and then inner voices would start up again, convincing me to close my heart down and protect it.

After many months of this inner war, I had to admit that my mind's idea of surrender was not going to work. My mind believed that surrender in my relationship meant letting go of all the thoughts and feelings that were making me miserable. This was logical and my devoted mind went to work on it immediately. But I discovered that my mind could only attempt such a shift with the inner agreement that I would be kept safe and protected under all circumstances. So the battle was never over; the resistance to the moment, to what *is*, was as strong as ever.

That realization led me to my heart and the possibility that I could have a different experience of surrender there. In the depths of my heart, I discovered that there is no danger, that I am completely safe and loved. My heart encouraged me not to "let go" but to feel everything fully; to give thoughts an opportunity to flow in and out; to continue the inquiry of the mind; to continually come back to the center of heart—the core of the Divine Feminine which knows that surrender is not about letting go; it is about embracing all there is.

My heart knows there is nothing to lose in any situation because radical love, open-hearted love, is the great unifier of all things and people. The Divine Feminine is unity. It brings all of Life together. When I used my mind without my heart the separation from others and the All seemed so real that at times I felt like ending my life; I could not bear the struggle anymore. When I began to go into the depths of my heart and continue to use the tools for the mind inquiry, I began to experience the great mystery of surrender. My head and heart had never been aligned before, and this new experience of alignment was at its core, the experience of surrender. I was free to come back home to the center of my being and live the unity of my body, mind and spirit.

The Mind That Resists Surrender

We undergo the alignment of head and heart through spiritual practice that expands the constricted heart and opens it to the All. The ego resists this surrender, preferring instead to keep the mind safe through the voices of reason and responsibility. It wants to have us believe that it alone can give us eternal happiness and self-worth. It pulls us out of unity and into separation, especially with our goals and dreams, and infiltrates our relationships to other, self and our feminine essence.

PROVING SELF

One common resistance to surrender is the ego voice that says, "Prove Yourself". This is the part of ego that believes in order to be worthy and to have a sense of purpose you must please others with all the skill, knowledge and charm you can muster up. In terms of relationship, women spend much time subconsciously trying to prove their worth. We do this sexually, intellectually, emotionally and through service, which usually comes with expectations of how others will receive us and our gifts. None of these ways are to be judged or condemned. Just notice as you go about your day, the subtle habits and behaviors that are designed to gain approval.

When I first began to look into my own desire to please, I was told that it was a "woman thing". I now believe that it is a "man thing" that has transmuted and shows its face in a different way for women. The need to please is based on the assumption that we must prove ourselves—which goes against every ounce of the Divine Feminine heart. It is an assumption that leads women to separate from themselves and buy into the belief that they are not worthy unless they "do" something that is considered to be of value by someone else. Both men and women experience the separation equally, but patriarchal notions make "proving" acceptable and "pleasing", not. One commands attention and is the energy of push; the other demands attention and is the energy of pull.

SACRED PRACTICE

💜 *Whether you engage in proving or pleasing, or a little of both, develop a habit to see from morning to evening what you think or do that brings your spirit outside of yourself in the hopes of being seen as worthy. Do you dress in a particular way for the sake of others? Do you communicate in different ways with different people, so that they will not reject you? Do you find yourself saying please and sorry more than necessary? Do you tell white lies and believe that it is for the good of all concerned? Whose approval are you hungry for? Who do you most want to control in order to keep yourself from feeling hurt or rejection?*

💜 *Now focus on your body. Where in your body can you feel the push of proving or the pull of approval? Go to that part of your body now and ask it what it wants to communicate to you. Accept whatever answer comes and bring the energy of the Divine Feminine love of your heart to that body part. Stay there until you feel the resistance dissolve. Resistance cannot remain in the powerful energy of the Divine Feminine, because it loves what is. It sees the real you, all of you, and loves it all equally.*

PERFECTING SELF

Many women and men hold onto the belief that they and others are flawed and must work hard to attain every goal and achieve every vision as planned. They often aim for perfection and believe goals are an indication of worth; nothing short of 100 percent achievement of these goals satisfies them. Success is measured in how closely they reach their own personal target.

Although definitions of success seem personal, many are the result of collective values and beliefs. Society dictates most goal setting, which includes earning high income, having "stuff", travelling the world and living a happily-ever-after fairytale relationship with a soul mate. People pay millions of dollars to hear others tell them how to live this dream—the dream of the collective. Perfection is perceived as this dream and it separates women from their intuitive hearts and Goddess energy. The heart of the Goddess does not concern itself with what is perfect and what is not because there is no judgment and no categorizing. When true surrender occurs there is only the unity of love.

I am not advocating for women to abandon goals and intentions. I am simply inviting a new level of consciousness in which women can feel free to love and accept what is, at every moment; a level of consciousness in which there is no need or desire to create a self image based on completion of The Dream. In a patriarchal society we are taught to list what we do as soon as we meet someone, and if we are at a networking function or cocktail party long enough, we will inevitably list accomplishments that prove our identity within what we do. Perhaps the "perfection" identity is go-getter, gifted, high achiever, expert, problem solver … whatever it is, it draws us from our hearts back into our conditioned minds. This makes surrender into our open hearts near impossible as we venture further and further away from the alignment of our heart and head.

Sacred Practice

As you go about your day, be aware of expectations of perfection or "doing better" whether the voices or feelings are positive or negative. Ask yourself why you have these expectations. Many of my students claim that nobody is harder on them than themselves. Ask yourself why that is. Then love the different personalities that are hard on you, bringing them to your Divine Feminine heart to be nurtured. Ask them to voice their concerns—hear the lesson behind the fearful message. Observe with gentleness and compassion and breathe into emotions, allowing them to pass through you like waves. Observe your state beyond the passing emotion and feel the clear space in your body where there is a peace that has always been with you and is now being unveiled.

Forgiveness: Human and Divine

While surrender is one secret to living in the Mother Heart, forgiveness is the other. Authentic forgiveness resides deep within our Mother Heart and is directly linked to the wisdom and experience of being one with God. It is activated by love. Superficial forgiveness, though, is fear-based and conditional upon a similar experience not occurring again. It makes us "feel good" that we have let go of a grudge or anger or vice but because of a deeper lack of self forgiveness, the heart closes again and again.

When forgiveness is authentic, it flowers from the open heart; as you feel yourself blooming open to love, you fully accept others because you fully accept yourself. And you fully accept yourself because you are connected to the sacred love that you are. As mentioned in the Virgin Heart chapters, connecting to self as sacred love is a spiritual discipline, and I believe that authentic forgiveness is part of this discipline. It is not as if we surrender, forgive and have compassion once and be done with it. As humans we are humbled by the lifelong process of committing to who we really are: love incarnate.

Eventually, as authentic forgiveness becomes a state that you experience more and more, it is no longer as most people would define it: Where I am letting go of something you have "done" to me. Now the practice is more about embracing compassion as a way of life; it is not so much a letting go of as it is the reciprocal energy of giving your heart. This energy of the giving heart is a gift for both you and another.

SELF FORGIVENESS

More than any other spiritual process, self forgiveness has been my personal challenge. As a young woman I based my worth on the tribe (family or co-workers or friends) being pleased or unhappy with my actions. I closed my heart to the "self" that felt rejection and then erased these memories along with the version of self connected to the memories. I am amazed how very little I remember about my life, even up to the age of thirty-five. I now believe that my default mechanism, learned when I was very young, was to block any form of trauma and even mild conflict that threatened to challenge the "good girl" I hoped to be; the one that made everyone happy.

After giving birth to two beautiful boys and helping women entrepreneurs become successful, I went through a period in my life where I did take on the identity of the Good Girl, and everyone was pleased with me. Life, in my eyes, had finally arrived! But as all illusions come to an end, so too did this. As both of my babies reached school age, my increasing strain with the people closest to me became more and more evident. When I announced that I was not willing to work out differences with my business partners and at the same time, announced I was separating from my husband, I realized that I had lost the "good girl" and would never get her back. While I understood she was a product of society and my own need to be liked I felt I could not live without her. After all, she listened to my harsh words; she gave me someone to lecture and rant and rave at. She was my scapegoat. Without her, who was I? Without her, I lost my identity.

It is a curious thing, the ability to forgive self. My realization was that I created a self that could never be fulfilled because she was made of other people's ideals, values and beliefs. She existed outside of me, and in my fortieth year, she said goodbye.

So, no more problems with forgiveness, right? Wrong! Since Good Girl was gone, I had to fill in the space she left behind. And that space was filled by another creation—the Woman of Despair. I now had someone to pity because she just couldn't help herself in a state of utter rejection by the people she loved. Eventually I felt bitter towards her too for not being the more masculine, take-action, get-it-done-under-all-odds sort of woman I needed to be.

The selves I created were always subject to a lack of forgiveness and never fulfilled the role that I had created for them.

A couple years later I discovered the freedom in releasing these roles and identity. In the space of day-to-day life, void of meaning-making, I could experience forgiveness without even needing to call it that. It was simply a quiet, serene softness that flowed into my body as a felt sense of acceptance.

Sacred Practice

💜 *Identify a personality type that you believe you have, or a set behavior. How do your friends or family describe you? How do these responses influence your self-acceptance or lack of self-acceptance?*

💜 *If you could isolate this identity as one aspect of self, what does this person look like in your mind, act like, think like? How much of this creation is yours and how much of it is based on the opinion of others?*

💜 *What stories about your life are connected to this identity? Do the stories help you to forgive self, or do they resist forgiveness?*

In my fortieth year, I resisted forgiveness by creating and recreating the story of what "really" happened in my marriage. Because of the identity and role I had created as Good Girl and Woman of Despair, I happily and unconsciously created stories that fit either one or the other, depending on who I was talking to. If I believed the person to be very loving and accepting, I found myself emphasizing that my soul could no longer be with this man, and although I would always love him, it was time to move on for the sake of both of us. It was as if we both knew deep in our hearts that a cycle of our life was complete. If the person I shared with was, in my perception, judgmental and rigid in their belief systems, I would simply say that communication was poor. If I was really brave or particularly angry I gave the image of the man in front of the TV connecting with his laptop and potato chips instead of me. Sharing my story with different people in different ways may seem manipulative and unspiritual, but I tell you this because in the depths of our challenges, each one of us engages in this behavior to some degree. We hold on to the good opinion of others by proving who we are—and we do that mainly through our stories.

In *Radical Forgiveness*, Colin Tipping suggests that part of the healing process around forgiveness is to indulge in your story and the feelings that arise as you tell the story; this can be done effectively and privately through writing. My separation with my husband brought out a full spectrum of emotions and stories. Some bits of journaling included: Why does he have to be so cold and unfeeling? It's his fault we ended up where we are and he just won't recognize it. Why can't I just have a normal life and stop making things so hard? Everything is my fault. I'm not fit for relationships. How dare he say that! I feel like my spirit has left me for good. I want to die. My body wants to leave this earth. I am trying to send love and it's so hard. Bring me peace dear God bring me peace....

Get it out in the open so that you can experience the other stages of healing. Without the initial feelings and stories, the process is at best a forced and shallow demonstration of forgiveness, where you are likely to be repeatedly triggered by a similar event or person and never experience the freedom that authentic forgiveness gifts you.

My story was told plenty of times before I was able to really feel the emotion hidden within it. Sometimes the emotion was anger; mostly, it was a feeling of profound sadness, a death, a loss of the highest magnitude. The loss was so great that tears seemed inadequate to lift it from my body. And that is why I needed the outlet of writing and speaking...until I no longer did.

When I did express anger, it taught me and healed me just as much as the sadness. While my Good Girl story usually involved feeling a lack of communication with my business partners and lack of intimacy with my husband, the Woman of Despair felt rage and aimed for the sympathy jugular, insisting that the others were to blame for the mess; that my emotional carnage was a direct result of their actions. The truth is, neither of these stories is fully true or fully false; nor does it matter to what extent. It matters that I now see that each version *is* a story, and that I choose to believe whatever fits my identity, roles and beliefs at that moment.

Inquiring into these thoughts and stories is one way to freedom and self acceptance. The way of the Divine Feminine is to bring every process back to the heart. So once you are finished inquiring, bring this version of self that you've held onto during your challenge, the one you have not forgiven, to your heart. Nurture, love and laugh at her humanity. Like Elizabeth Lesser says, we are all "bozos on the bus" and have astonishingly similar challenges and ways of dealing with those challenges. The saving grace is to come back to your heart with the "bozo" knowing that she will be loved and cared for; that she is allowed to make mistakes, show emotion and have thoughts and actions that are out of integrity. Sometimes that is the one wake-up call that brings us home to the heart; deeply, richly and satisfyingly home.

Forgiving the "Dark" Side

There are times when we feel that what we have said or done is unforgiveable and that we truly ought to pay for what we've done. And we make ourselves pay for it by a lack of self love. Each of us has our own barometer as to what is unforgiveable—usually based on the Velcro Voices of our personalities. For me the unforgiveable was leaving my marriage: the good girl stays, the good mother stays, the faithful servant should listen to the call of duty. The more I was unable to accept myself and my decisions, the more I acted in ways that hurt people. Sometimes, I could hardly believe that the very things that enraged me about my husband were also within me. I did not want to see we were mirrors for each other.

The good news is that in every dark moment, in every act that resists our truth as Divine Beings of Light, there is the opportunity to undergo what Elizabeth Lesser calls "The Phoenix Process". We can die and be born again from the very ashes that destroy us. Some days, the only thing that got me up in the morning was reminding myself of this. Our bodies can "rebirth" into love again and again. We can remember who we really are by simply acknowledging that we can choose again. And in making a Light choice, our shadow is embraced as our step towards light, rather than the descent into hell.

My story is not a fairytale ending and there are still days when I weep with regret over what I could have done, should have said, or might have become. Yet I know that in my darkest deeds, the times when I was furthest from my heart-opening essence, I learned what love is. I learned most what love is when I was furthest from my Divine Feminine Heart. I learned most to honor all of life when I acted in ways that dishonored my family or friends. I learned most to respect myself when I chose not to listen to my deepest soul truth. I learned most to be gentle with others when I aggressively acted from my anxiety. Not everyone learns and I don't pretend that each learning is a permanent step towards enlightenment. But I can choose again and there is great freedom in this choice. It is the freedom of a heart open to Life and all its light and shadow gifts.

Self Forgiveness and Physical Healing

Many new age and channeled books claim that the woman Mary was a profound healer just like her son and had great wisdom and skill in assisting with the healing of physical ailments, emotional challenges and spiritual dark nights of the soul. I have no doubt this is true as the testimonies throughout the centuries tell of experiences of Mary as the healer of the heart; the encourager of forgiveness, the lover of gentleness.

One message Mary has repeatedly given people around the world during visitations or channelings is to love one another and have compassion. This message is vital as we head into a time where we are physically and metaphorically entering a new era—the era of human consciousness and the dignity of the human heart. Western culture suppresses and minimizes the vast wisdom of the heart, favoring the mind that can be used to conquer and achieve. Fortunately, the Divine Feminine has been kept alive in many indigenous cultures. The honoring of the heart that *is* the feminine essence of divinity can only survive where the people are trained to listen to the cycles and rhythms of all that is natural—the body, the earth, the spirit. The illusions of the mind do not dominate the honoring of the natural state of body and spirit.

From my own experience, my physical challenges have been healed through a return to this natural state in which I love all parts of me and honor all aspects of my human and divine self. Self forgiveness is embracing my Virgin Heart, Mind and Body as the Divine Feminine essence. It brings home to my heart all of the aspects of me that I could never fully accept or understand. In terms of healing, forgiveness is truly a mystical act; it is not one that can be done solely with the mind. Mostly, it is not even a reasonable act; depending on the severity of the circumstance, our minds could never tackle the mountain of hurt alone. Just as there are spontaneous healings, which Mary is renowned for at sacred sites around the world, there is also such a thing as spontaneous forgiveness—it happens when we surrender to the miracle beyond our mind, beyond our body, beyond anything we have ever known or will know while on this earth. It is the feminine love presence fully becoming one with you.

FORGIVING ANOTHER

True freedom isn't simply 'I'm free.'
True freedom is 'Everything is free.'
Adyashanti

I have been fortunate in my lifetime to have many opportunities to forgive. I say this sincerely because it is the people who challenge our self love, testing it to make it stronger, that are indeed our soul mates. I often tell people my belief about soul mates is different from what they will read in romance novels: our soul mates truly teach us what love is by strengthening our muscle of forgiveness. They may be our lovers but they could be our sister, friend, co-worker or a stranger.

For me, nothing has been more challenging than letting go of wanting for or wishing for people to be other than what they are. It is easy in the short term to try and control others with our behavior, beliefs, requests and demands. But it is far easier in the long run to let them be who they are without imposing our will to change them. In allowing others to be who they are, we become radical love—the unconditional love we want to experience.

I know this is far easier said than done. For many months I heard Guidance say, "Bring him to me," and knew that the only way to bring anyone to God was indeed to let them be free; to surrender my will to see a particular outcome. In this case, the voice was relentless, repeating itself daily. At last I began a spiritual practice of sending the energy of love from my heart and cutting any energetic chords of fear and attachment with the assistance of Archangel Michael. I became aware of my mind's manipulation, trying to control the situation and person in a myriad of ways. Each time, I simply observed the thoughts that ran away with my spirit. I became familiar with the feeling of this running away and then became attuned to the feeling of releasing this fear-based energy. Finally, I grew into the surrender of a service that unifies: I felt love and gratitude for the lessons I was learning and for the soul mate relationship itself. It was not easy; but the discipline of acting consistently in this way gave me great freedom that I knew was freedom for all. I believe that when we free everyone and everything around us we find true freedom for ourselves.

A friend of mine, whose beloved had ended their relationship, spent many months wishing and hoping for her outcome, her needs and her desires to be met. Once she practiced releasing with radical love, her world changed and she became serene and truly blessed her former lover through the energy of her thoughts, prayers and feelings. While I was staying with her, the lover wrote to her that he wanted to be with her that night. She tells me that they now enjoy their time together and feel every moment yet neither one is attached to their relationship looking a certain way, nor do they have a need to define their roles within it. They are living the Virgin moment and are embracing the freedom that comes with that. As author Byron Katie says, they are "Loving What Is".

SACRED PRACTICE

♥ *Think of a situation where you are challenged to love another or to accept them fully the way that they are. Now visualize yourself taking this person into a dungeon, handcuffed, and locking the door and walking away. Feel the panic and pain of the other as you begin walking. Hear your name being called out in desperation. Imagine the fear and rejection as the person continues to call out your name. Feel what it feels like to continue walking. To turn your back. Where do you feel this in your body? What does it feel like? Is it moving or steady? Light or heavy? What color and size is it? Stay with this feeling for a few minutes.*

♥ *As you continue walking in the dungeon, you notice another cell around the corner and hear the sobbing of a woman. As you near this cell, you see that it is you, and you are holding a baby. This baby is also crying. She is also you. The woman calls out to you, begging you to open the lock of the cell door. The baby calls out to you, wailing in the energy of fear. But you choose to continue walking, to turn your back on Mother and Child. Notice the feeling in your body now.*

Where do you feel this in your body? What does it feel like? Is it moving or steady? Light or heavy? What color and size is it? Stay with this feeling for a few minutes.

♥ *Now return to Mother and Child, opening the lock and freeing them. Imagine that you hold both of them in your arms, with a deep care and compassion that grows and grows until the whole dungeon is filled with the color and size of this love. You bring Mother and Child into the core of your heart where they are safe and nurtured in the eternal light of the divine. Saturate your whole being in this feeling.*

♥ *With Mother and Child in your heart, you again hear the shouting of the person you left handcuffed in a cell. You reach for the lock and as you open the cell, you continue to feel the love that surrounds you and the love within you, and you know at once that nothing can harm you ever again. You unlock the handcuffs and open the dungeon door, watching this guest walk away freely, never to return. As you watch, you are aware of a shift in your body. What does it feel like? Is it moving or steady? Light or heavy? What color and size is it?*

♥ *Repeat this visualization with anyone or any situation that you need to forgive or that you need to surrender to. Be sure to feel the Mother Love as part of every visualization. As my friend and Master Rebirther, Mahara Brenna says, "There is a point in spiritual practice, where the love of the Love grows." We want to get back to the Mother Heart where we have always been loved and where we will always be love. Surrender and forgiveness are paths to open the expansiveness of this heart and return to the majesty of our Sacred Feminine essence.*

Meditative Reflections
for the Mother Heart

- ♥ I am free. Everything is free.

- ♥ I accept and love myself. I accept and love others.

- ♥ New life is waiting in the ashes of surrender.

5

GODDESS ENERGY

A woman walks into my spiritual writer's group one evening, and I am immediately drawn to her energy; I cannot name it, yet it is familiar. Perhaps this is the mystical energy of the Goddess. She does not have to say or do anything in particular—both men and women recognize Her. What is this recognition? What makes us drawn to her, fascinated by her nature? My mind begins to search for the answer, and my heart whispers, "You already know. Feel it within."

Popular, historical and literary images of the Goddess partially explain her powerful energy and presence. There is the seductive Goddess known through film and media, the Goddess connected to nature and creation, the various athletic, wise and powerful Goddesses of Greek mythology, and the many Goddesses connected to spiritual traditions, such as Kali in India, Tara in Tibet and Kuan Yin in China. These Goddesses are known in the form of spirit and many people around the world connect to their strength and compassion. Mary is rare in that she represents the merging

111

of both the human and divine Goddess. She transcended the human condition while being an Earth Mother who was in service to those in need; as a Divine Mother, she is known in apparitions and visitations to be the all powerful healer and giver of radical love. Two powerful Goddess images of Mary are the Black Madonna of Czestochowa and Our Lady of Guadalupe; through both, she is known for her strength amidst suffering, her compassion for all of life and her call to gather and unite a world that separates from others and itself.

When I contemplate Mary as Goddess and witness a Goddess as I did that night at my writing group, I see that there is no concern for pleasing others and much concern for loving others. This is the difference: the energy of the Goddess comes within her center, her soul, and pours out love that is contained there; she loves because she is love. The outside world has no hold on her, and while she can choose to be "nice", it is not a choice that is based on societal norms, expectations and patriarchal good girl images. It is a choice that flows from the expression of love that she is.

I believe that this Divine Love is deeply integrated in the Goddess heart, mind and spirit, and is sometimes referred to as self love, although it is not the traditional understanding of self love. The self help version of self love deals with the ego aspect of self and the esteem of the ego. Esteem building can be a useful ongoing process, yet tending to spiritual practice is what brings woman into her own wisdom. This wisdom produces a confidence that transcends outward appearance and becomes the very fabric of her body, heart, mind and spirit. She does not need to boast, or use her gifts to persuade or inspire; her in-spirit presence touches the hearts of all who meet her.

Woman is born Goddess. She forgets this as she integrates into society and adopts belief systems that say wisdom and worth are to be found outside of her body and mind. Often decades later, through breaking down and then breaking open, she emerges from the cocoon of illusion to become the beautiful butterfly that is her truth. She is free at last to experience herself as the love that she spent her life looking for.

How does she taste this freedom; how does she come to experience herself as this love? I believe it involves the collective evolution of the Divine Feminine within us; the Madonna Code does not contain one answer, yet, the answer exists everywhere. It cannot be "found" because it is already here, within and around us. There is no need to search for something that was never lost. Yet it is our purpose during this crucial time in history to reclaim the love that we are. Part of that journey may be the experience of temporarily leaving the spirit that houses our hearts and bodies.

JOURNAL INSIGHTS: TAMING THE WAR WITHIN

I am calling my spirit back from a mission that it has gone on—a mission to be attached to something other than the love that I am; a mission to prove that I am separate; a mission to prove that someone else is separate from me. It is a gift, this awareness, because I look into the deepest beliefs about who I am and am now willing to release these beliefs. I am tired of the drama, the resistance, the fighting of my ego against love energy. My desire to end the war within is intense; I no longer want to be actively involved on earth. Please, I pray, make me an angel. I want to soothe the voices that claim me; with heavenly arms I want to embrace them and stop pushing them away. I want to soften the edges of my ego. I am tired and sleep as much as I can; I notice a loss of interest in the things that once gave me life. This too is part of my journey to reclaim my spirit.

CALLING OUR SPIRIT BACK

Calling our spirit back involves a shift in perception and a deeper look into the ego self and how it commands our spirit. I asked questions when I felt I was not a good mother and not reliable in providing for my family. I realized the expectations I had around mothers and around money and began to simplify my beliefs about both into single statements. What was my relationship to mother and money? "I am not good enough" and "I am not financially successful doing what I love to do" were two core beliefs that carried my spirit away on missions of fear, suspicion, uncertainty and even, at times, vengeance. After all, I reasoned, someone needs to pay for the state I ended up in!

I realized that these voices were mostly the child within that desperately wants to do the right thing and wants above all to be liked, loved and accepted. I needed to feel into the mature heart within to embrace this child, inquire into the lies and message she was telling me and release the castle of illusion she lived in. When I began a daily practice of calling my spirit back from these beliefs and asking the questions that my ego self didn't want to reflect on, I slowly released the resistance and entered into the heart of the Goddess.

This practice of releasing resistance and calling my spirit back was the beginning of the end of suffering. It heightened sensitivity to my body's wisdom: feeling the leaving of spirit and the re-entry of spirit as a very tangible force. I now understand that my energy field, the electromagnetic field around me, is powerful when I return to the heart of the Goddess, the truth of who I am.

During this withdrawal the resistance softened and dissolved; I began the lifelong journey of the Observer, lovingly hearing the voices of my conditioning and core beliefs as a compassionate third party. This Observer was not bowing out of life and removing me from working through challenges; she was able to help me see the voices as one aspect of my ego, not the reality of who I am. And part of my process with her was to lovingly ask myself questions; to inquire into the voices that wore me down so thoroughly.

Sacred Practice

Take a few moments each day and bring your awareness to your body. Ask, "What part of me is off with someone else? What part of me has attached to a person because of a belief or fear I have not released? What part of me feels empty and where is the fullness?"

Caroline Myss says that if we don't heal our history, if we don't engage in processes like calling our spirit back, there is very little energy left for creation. In fact, Myss calculates that as little as 2% of our total energy is available for creation, and 98% is consumed by our past unexamined and unhealed experiences. Imagine the life force that runs through a Goddess who has called her spirit back! This is the life force that is the undefinable essence of attraction. The Universe and all creatures honor the Goddess because it is her centered, present moment strength of spirit that blooms the world into love.

Journal Insights: A Conversation with God

Today I asked for a miracle. "I need a miracle," I cried. I really need a miracle."

"You are the miracle," God answered.

THE GODDESS AND THE UNDERWORLD: THE GIFT OF ADDICTION

In calling my spirit back, I was willing at last to look at the possibility that I was addicted. To me, this word once took on frightening connotations of being a slave to a substance; I believed it was not part of my personal experience. As I entered the process of retrieving my spirit, I was humbled by my inner wisdom to be shown the extent to which I had become addicted to the acceptance and approval of others. This was magnified by my shame of being a woman who chose divorce. Anyone who was part of my tribe could bring me down with a single word or gesture, proving my lack of worth. During this time, one woman held me as I broke down and broke open; she showed me that the very addiction I was part of was the experience that would save me.

Nancy Kerner is a Goddess that emerged through a Phoenix process, wrapping the ashes of her own addiction into a gift, first for herself and then for others. In an intimate conversation with Nancy, she revealed to me the unfolding of the gift:

Addiction ultimately led to the awakening of my consciousness. Addictions of all types can cause emotional and energetic imbalances within body, mind and spirit. They can keep a conscious lifestyle elusive at best and at worst keep the addict in a perpetual unconscious state completely unaware that any alternatives exist. My Higher Self was trying to guide me back to my consciousness where I'd find the Source of my true power with Spirit.

All of us are born in and as pure consciousness. We all lose the essence of that consciousness when our spirit becomes wounded or hurt. I became acutely unconscious at a very young age. Drama and chaos in my home was intense. I adopted a sugar bowl as my first addiction. I unconsciously felt that it somehow created some distance between me and my current reality. Later on in life, the sugar bowl was replaced with drugs and alcohol.

There are many roads to consciousness and a lot of them are paved with tragedy or near tragedy, sometimes in the form of an "accident". My story is rooted in a near tragic version. It was an accident that involved a close family member who escaped with a one-week stay in the hospital. The event took me out of toxic family dynamics and gave me the opportunity to connect with Source. I asked, "Is there a God? What do you look like? How do I know you're there?" The answer was profound and was delivered as though my asking had been expected for some time. My counselor called it a 'coinciGod'. Never before had I experienced an asking and a giving at immediate speed. Within the first few months of recovery my intuition was waking up and growing. There is no doubt in my mind that it was a conscious connection—a conversation with Source. It would take time to accept the wisdom, and I began reading everything I could on spirituality. It led me to a path specific to women and the topics that women are passionate about.

I was getting the message, "You will work with women around the world". How would I do that? I couldn't even complete a sentence without crying. Yet the voice told me not to worry and took me to women who took me to my body. They said listen to intuition, trust your feelings—although men said the opposite. I wasn't sure what to trust because men told me to be on time, show up, have an agenda, know your goals. Each woman has her own inner guidance, and once I let go and started trusting that, I found another realm of living that was more about allowing. I found that women would sit in circles and take turns sharing from the heart.

When we are called into consciousness, no matter the catalyst, (birth, death, loss, addiction) we are being called to take our power back.

Nancy helped me see that my addiction to acceptance and approval was a call for me to take my power back—to call my spirit home. Her gentle wisdom and the women gathered in circle guided me in that journey. We shared our deepest passions, fears, emotions and love. Each week we began to trust more and more, to open to our Divine Feminine hearts and feel what it was like to be in pure feminine essence. This opening is what it means to take back power—it is a oneness rather than a winning; it claims the self, rather than conquering the self; it is the whole of love, found again, rather than the parts of love that need fixing. It is the return of the Goddess.

TRUST AND THE GODDESS

A big part of my journey into the heart of the Goddess is self trust. As I wrote this book and felt my life dissolving personally and professionally, I knew that I needed to experience it as part of who I am.

As with self love, I think we are trained to believe that if we could just have self trust everything would be ok. The reason that most people never reach self love or never experience trust in themselves, is because they enter into an unspoken agreement that comes from ego. This agreement goes something like this: "I, your ego, want you to be in control and have confidence that you can control your world, yourself, your body, your emotions and, most of all, the actions of other people. This is the only way that you will ever learn to trust yourself, by doing, doing, doing. Work at controlling your life! You cannot trust the outside world; they can betray you at any moment, so you must control them in order to feel self trust. Stay in the future and think about the past to control your life while you take massive action to achieve your goals on your terms. These are the secrets to self trust."

Heart-wisdom laughs at these messages, knowing them as the Velcro Voices of conditioned mind. These voices are often loud and overbearing, yet the heart is willing to speak truth if you become very still. It may sound something like this: "Be still and know that I am God. Feel into me. You are the love that you seek. You are the miracle you are asking for. All is here now. Be still." As is common with the heart, it speaks simply, quietly, concisely. The less words, the more likely your heart is communicating with you. The more stillness and pure feeling beyond fear-based emotion, the more you experience this wisdom. Self trust definitions dissolve into this feeling; you are centered and one with God.

When you recognize this level of self trust, you will want to be of service to other women who will be changed

forever by your presence. Women need other women to
bring them back to the Divine Feminine—not by telling
them what to do, but by being present with them,
accepting and loving them, giving them a voice and giving
them the gift of listening to another woman. Nancy
Kerner holds the space for this to happen through her
women's circles. I asked Nancy how self trust returns as
she witnesses the miracles that take place in women's
circles. She shared with me these thoughts:

> Trust is the foundation of any relationship. We create
> this foundation by being in a healthy circle of women.
> Women take turns listening with her ears, eyes and
> with the energy that is flowing within her body, as she
> learns how to trust her body's intuition. I ask the
> women, "How does your gut feel when someone is
> talking?" In circles of women we teach the young
> women where their power is. Our intention is to create
> communities that bring new experiences for them to
> practice trusting themselves and being comfortable in a
> community of women. We do this by asking them to
> bring the food, decorate the room and assign volun-
> teer positions. These are life-enhancing opportunities
> where women learn to trust themselves and the other
> women. They see the women who are leaders and
> watch how they communicate. In loving, spiritual
> communities of women there are lots of hugs, kisses
> and a welcoming feeling.

> I ask women to pay attention to how they are
> bringing themselves into circles and events. I ask
> them, "Can you trust yourself to show up and do
> what you say you will do?" Women often change their
> minds a lot moving from one thing to another and

too much 'flow' can be a seen as being too flighty or undependable. A powerful leader learns to match her actions to her words. When she commits to being at an event, for example, for every minute she's late, she'll miss vital teachings and lessons. People notice if a woman is habitually late and she becomes known for it, and that can break down her ability to be trusted with important details or tasks later on. We like to say, "Don't be on time to events, be early." That way everyone's experience is shared from the beginning to the end. Being on time creates the foundation of trust for the circle. It's not about being rigid and cancelling out the beauty of being in flow— rather it's about a commitment to practice building that foundation of trust in all that we co-create.

Another element of self trust is knowing our innate gifts. Nancy says,

How can we trust ourselves if we don't know what our gifts are? We learn what they are by being in circles and communities of women. We are constantly learning new gifts and creating new experiences that go along with bringing our innate gifts to the world. Ask yourself, "How can I give my gift and be of service to humanity in some small way?" When you feel good giving your gift in that way, then you'll be able to give it in a bigger way later on. Be patient with the Divine Timing of knowing when and where to give your gifts. The most important element is to keep asking where you can be in service in the moment. Stay fully conscious and present so you can hear the answer.

Nancy says it's not necessary to immediately know your gifts, and that part of the struggle for many women in discovering their gifts is their self-judgment:

Women second guess themselves and need to hear that it's okay to make mistakes; that's how we learn. Women are often very hard on themselves and need to practice being sweet and gentle with self. Look for a woman who lives a life that you admire and if you can, learn from her. Seek a healthy woman who will take you under her wing as a mentor with the heart of a mother. Accept and trust your mentor to show you your gifts. And if you are the mentor, show women the beauty of what you see in them. A powerful mentor is a woman who naturally finds the good in someone and will lovingly point out the energy leaks that keep them stuck in old outdated patterns. She does this with as much love and kindness as she can. However, we are all having this human experience, so be responsible for your own actions and remember that she is just like you; doing the best she can with what she knows in this moment. When she knows how to respond differently, she will. Give her permission to make mistakes too. A wise woman will continue to take new risks of exposing herself and being vulnerable with her heart.

Doubt

When I cannot trust myself I know the signs: procrastination, lack of focus and lack of direction. I am easily distracted by chaos around me and if there is no chaos, I create chaos. I sabotage myself, not doing what needs to be done because at a very deep level I doubt my worth, my skill, my ability. It is easier to prove that I am right about my lack of aptitude than to sit with my heart that knows the truth of the great Goddess power.

This power is tucked away as I leave my inner strength and wisdom, and attach to someone or something outside of me. The sparkling drama of the outer life pulls me along with its suffering and emotional upheaval. I go willingly because it doesn't demand that I believe in myself and look within at my doubt. Because my energy is directed at people and events, I soothe myself by taking a course and buying another book in the hopes of dealing with the chaos.

While in workshops and researching different resources, I focus on healing my trust with people who are close to me. I develop a passionate will to trust them, ruminating and deconstructing relationships, taking the focus off self and onto the other person. I believe I am doing great work on myself, and that this will lead to healing once and for all. I praise my resiliency to the challenges in my life. Yet this proud resiliency is an attempt to control my heart's wisdom. A wisdom that whispers, "Look within."

Resiliency of the soul is to stand naked and vulnerable, surrendering to the journey within. Surrendering to self trust again and again. Surrendering to a remembrance of that which we are. Sometimes that means accepting and experiencing fully that which we are not. In embracing all and loving what is, a sense of trust is natural, not forced, not dependent on achievements and praise.

SACRED PRACTICE

♥ *To begin the journey of self trust, scan your body and discover where trust lives. What color is it? What size? What is the texture and shape? How does it feel in your body? Sit with the feeling of trust. Have you felt this feeling before? Ask this area of your body to give you a message about what it needs from you right now. Record this in a journal and revisit the exercise once a week for a few weeks, documenting awareness of your body trust.*

♥ *With your journal, inquire into habits that keep you from trusting yourself and trusting in the divine. What takes you away from center? What chaos do you find yourself getting into? What distractions do you immerse yourself in and why?*

INTUITION

Intuition is the mother of all inspired action, all love-based creation. It does not come from reason—that is why it has been rejected in the patriarchal western world. Patriarchy has tried long and hard to rid the world of this Divine feminine force precisely because it will in part, always be the unknowable, the uncontained, the wild flow that is Goddess. The limitless, boundless aspect of intuition, feminine by nature, has frightened many men since the beginning of time because they try to understand it with their logical brain. Because intuition is also the ultimate reminder that we are One with God, it can be difficult to embrace. After all, that would mean access to unlimited potential, authentic love-power and sacred wisdom. And that scares people.

SACRED PRACTICE

💜 *If you are scared or intuition is a mystery for you, be still and quiet, listen to your feelings and all of your five senses, allowing them to flow through your body. Bring to your awareness a decision you are about to make, preferably one that doesn't involve strong fear, and feel both choices in your body. When I write two truths and two illusions, holding one in each hand, not knowing which is which, I can tell which one is truth by paying attention to the feeling in my body. If it physically feels lighter and happier, I know I am holding a Truth. Yet when I hold what is not true, feelings of anger, hopelessness, even physical heaviness come upon me, as though I am entering a mild depression.*

💜 *Experiment how Truth and its absence affect your body. Dr. David Hawkins, author of* Power vs. Force: The Hidden Determinants of Human Behavior, *demonstrates that we can experiment with words, thoughts and images to show how Truth is connected organically to our bodies. By holding a thought in our mind, a message in our hand, or a picture against our solar plexus, our bodies weaken with illusion and lack of love and strengthen when the Truth of love is in its presence.*

It is helpful to know that Truth can come to us in different forms. Most of us have a predominant way in which we receive guidance. Clairvoyants are visual and see their guidance in their third eye (just above and between your eyes, in the mind). Others hear a voice that clearly directs and supports them. Some sense temperature and pressure shifts in the air and feel their body receive God-bumps and tingling. Others have none of these experiences, but have a gut sense; they just know, without knowing how they know. Regardless of the way you receive guidance there are many resources to help you strengthen this skill (and it is a skill, not a gift for a chosen few). The biggest help for me is to keep my heart open to Life and all the forms in which it communicates, to be aware of any thoughts of doubt and to only speak in a way that honors my feminine capacity to know what the Divine is telling me. These practices all strengthen my unity with the heart of the Goddess within.

The more you practice opening your heart to all there is, both what your ego mind deems acceptable and that which it rejects, the more your intuition flourishes. Your ego begins to know that the higher self, or the soul, is in charge, and with this Divine Leadership, there is nothing that intuition can give us that is too scary or too overwhelming. It is the safest place to be because you are in the arms of Love, being directed and guided on your soul's journey.

Four Blocks to Intuition

If people have no loving relationship to their intuition, they generally don't trust it. Many women have been schooled in institutions where left-brained activity is praised and creative, spontaneous right-brained activity is not valued because it is not quantifiable. Some women are exposed to religious institutions that insist intuition can't be trusted as a Divine Source; that we must look outside of ourselves for the answers and that a specific religious leader will "handle" our intuition for us because we are not capable of managing it (and if we did manage it, we might use it to harm the beliefs and traditions long held sacred by these religions). This block is largely unconscious but is a powerful suppressed voice of the collective fear: we cannot trust ourselves with innate power.

SACRED PRACTICE

What are your beliefs about intuition? What is your first thought when others tell you that they have a gut sense, a knowing, a feeling about something? Do you support their way of knowing? How do you feel when you share that you have had an intuitive experience? Are you confident and comfortable? Embarrassed or anxious?

A second block is that people are afraid to be wrong or take intuitive advice and not have it lead to their vision of success. The core belief is that, "I'm not enough", so it's safer to stay where I am than listen to this intuition. When your intuition tells you to leave a relationship, or a job, for instance, most people won't listen until fate intervenes: you end up with an illness that forces you to stay home from work or you discover that your partner has been underhanded financially. We choose our destiny by following intuition or we can wait for fate to intervene. Go peacefully or go kicking and screaming, but go you must.

Sometimes the will to delve into intuition can be an act of ego just as much as the resistance to listening to it. In my observations through my spiritual events business, people who sign up for lectures and workshops about intuition tend to be in one of two groups: the first group are those who want to develop a more intimate connection to the feminine face of God and learn to surrender to its eternal force within them. They are there with love-based energy and tend to look radiant and calm. The other group is there with fear-based energy and want intuition to help them control their lives. They believe that this power or knowledge will stop them from suffering. And no doubt, there are times when intuition provides this. Each of us, however, has a contract that involves learning about life through challenges; through making unhelpful choices and developing unhelpful habits. Some of the most gifted intuitives are people who suffered the most horrific circumstances. Intuition grows each time we listen to its loving voice, but it is not meant to keep us from learning the lessons we've come here to learn.

SACRED PRACTICE

Ask yourself, "Which group am I mostly in, when it comes to wanting to develop intuition? Do I feel the will to control my life, or do I trust that guidance is designed to help me return to love regardless of what that may look like in my life circumstances?

A third block involves identity. When people are attached to their identity they resist the leap of faith that intuition demands of them. This was the case for me as a wife. I could not imagine myself as a single woman, a single mother and the single friend of married couples—single was not part of my identity. I heard the voice and felt the emptiness but I wanted the voice of the Divine to match the conditioned voice that defined "Karen" as anything but single! I trusted more in concepts my mind had constructed long ago than I did the ancient wisdom of my heart that has known me for eternity.

A final block is wondering what to do with the intuitive message once received—it seems that it is one thing to receive it and another to put it into reality. After months of agony, I finally had the courage to tell my husband the truth. The pain of keeping silent became greater than the benefits of holding on to the past and my identity as wife. We were at a Wayne Dyer talk and a 15-minute intermission had just started. I could not lift my leaden body off the seat to go and take a break with all the excited people in the auditorium. The words on my tongue were so waited with months of anxiety and tears that I could no longer bear to keep silent. "I think we should separate." Five words, an eternity of loss echoing through me. I felt nothing. It was as if the Universe was devoid of emotion and I was part of the great cosmos uttering Truth.

It was not long after that my Monkey Mind began saying, "So what next? What do I need to do? Will I be okay? What do I need to tell my kids? What about my aging mother, how will she handle it? Please just tell me what to do!" The anxiety of not knowing set in and I wanted intuition to give me a full-scale plan to protect my family and keep their hearts safe.

What I have learned in my communication with Mary, ascended masters and angels is that they very rarely give us the Big Picture and if we happen on occasion to receive it, the steps will not be downloaded all at once! The steps arrive in Divine Timing. Your only job is to take the first step. Have faith that once you act on this step you will be guided to the next. I wish I had trusted in this and really known it in my heart; with so much stress about not knowing the outcome, I blocked much of the guidance I otherwise would have received.

I often think back to what it must have been like for Mary to see and hear the angel Gabrielle and say "Yes", to full-heartedly accept her role as the mother of Christ. She was not told a hundred steps to prepare for this journey; neither was she given the big picture in any detail. She did have faith and hope that guidance would come when it was needed.

Part of the Goddess Heart is being strong in the not knowing; this is a trust in the feminine heart that is comfortable with the ways of mystery. Without it we couldn't grow in trust, surrender and forgiveness; we would trust only because we have been given a plan; we would surrender only because we know the outcome, and we would forgive only if the outcome and plan to get there met our expectations. The true value of these spiritual love actions would be lost on us. The Goddess heart knows that intuition is not a tool to predict the future in order to ease fear-based reality; it is a gift that directs us in this moment to express our love in ways that nurture and support our soul's growth. It is the love connection to All That Is.

JOURNAL INSIGHTS:
WHEN INTUITION AND OUTCOME MEET

As I write this book, I am at an Angel Empowerment Practitioner's retreat led by Cindy Smith. My shoulder has been aching for a couple of months and Cindy intuits anger lodged in my shoulder joint. I feel this as my truth, and we work to remove this energy. Later that night, I am stunned to discover that much of my anger comes from the outcome of following my guidance. My frustrations with my life as a single woman and single mom left me unconsciously bitter towards the intuition that guided me to separate from my husband.

It was also intuition that brought me deeper into self inquiry, to discover both my humanity and my divinity as never before. It was what brought me to enter into spiritual teaching and healing. With this arrive doubts of not being enough—Velcro Voices that try to convince me that the professor's paycheck that I could have had teaching in a university would be safe and stable. What did I think I was doing listening to my body, the whispering, the relentless images and sensations? Why not provide my family with security and the scholarly identity they could be certain and proud of?

After my healing with Cindy, I also saw that it is my feminine, or non-dominant side of my body that attracted pain over the past two years. The shoulder pain would return with my current perceptions: my joints in my arm would continue to scream until I let go of punishing my obedient heart.

I am ready now to fall in love with my feminine heart wisdom again, to be gentle with this most precious and Divine Source.

Intuition is one of the most revered and most feared aspects of the Goddess. Although we can take logical and reasonable steps to become more intuitive, the greatest gift we can give ourselves is to be intimately connected with our feminine hearts. When the Goddess is completely open to love and trusting of self and the Divine she bridges humanity and divinity with ease, grace and sacred wisdom. She is the Light, and her presence illuminates a path, inviting the Lover of all that is.

MEDITATIVE REFLECTIONS
FOR THE GODDESS HEART

- ♥ I love and bless my feminine heart wisdom.

- ♥ I trust the will of the Divine; I trust myself.

- ♥ Self Love is Divine Love.

❧ 6 ❧

THE GODDESS
AS LOVER

IN THE MANY FORMS THAT GODDESS shows up in the world, she is portrayed as a powerful, centered, wise and loving Divine Being. At one time, humans revered her as the feminine face of God and saw Her as the Creator of All. In fact, Goddess worship is one of the oldest forms of spiritual tradition, one that was healthy and alive prior to the introduction of the male dominated forms of God. Part of this healthy worship was honoring and respecting the female form, sensuality and powerful sexual essence. The Goddess was the natural lover, creating and integrating with all of Life. Now, despite the resurgence of the feminine over the last few years, Goddess images of sensuality and sexuality remain separate from Goddess as sacred and holy.

While Mary as the Virgin and Mother seems to be far removed from the world of Goddess as Lover, she is in my opinion, a powerful representation of someone who bridged humanity and divinity—the core of sacred intimacy. Mary is, as Andrew Harvey says of Jesus, "The

Lover of Lovers". She knows the trials of love and transcended earth-bound suffering through surrender, compassion and forgiveness. She returns us relentlessly to the feeling of love inside our hearts, no matter what the circumstance.

There are many processes available to love self and have an intimate relationship with a beloved. Some of these books and audio guides are transformational when you follow the steps for self exploration and connection with another. This book, however, challenges you to go beyond the "plan" and become the very qualities of love that you desire in another. It follows Mary energy, that invites both a merging of self with the Divine and self with another. The essence of this unification is love. There are hundreds of different forms of love, and in my experience, two of these forms embody the Goddess as Lover: joy and peace.

Dr. David Hawkins, through his muscle testing research, discovered that the forms of love containing the highest vibration of energy are joy and peace. I had the great privilege of meeting Dr. Hawkins at a Hay House conference and his presence changed my life forever. While I admired his book, *Power vs. Force,* and had an intellectual understanding of the work he devoted much of his life to, I did not understand it from my heart wisdom. That all changed while I was sitting in my conference chair waiting for his arrival.

I suddenly felt Spirit rock my body and the air around me. I turned around and at the far back of the ballroom I could see that he had come through the doors. As he slowly walked up an aisle he began to touch people, and as he did, many of them cried. One woman's tears silently streamed down her face as he touched the crown of her head, holding his palm there for a few precious moments. The closer he came to the area I was sitting the stronger the God presence in my body.

I imagined that this is what it must have been like for the open-hearted women who felt the presence of Jesus as he travelled by foot across the countryside. It was said that Jesus and Buddha could not hide from others. As they travelled into the depths of the hills and forests, people would find them because their love energy was so high that those open to its force would be drawn like a magnet. Many women living in those times were also avatars, including Mother Mary and Mary Magdalene, yet patriarchal recording of history limits our experience of them. We are told of their suffering and compassion yet rarely of the one quality of love that magnetizes the people to them: these avatars were lovers of joy and ascended during their life to become joy, the ultimate expression of loving all that is.

¶LOVERS OF ¶OY

In *Power vs. Force*, Dr. Hawkins explains the progression toward a state of joy:

> As Love becomes more and more unconditional, it begins to be experienced as inner Joy. This isn't the sudden joy of a pleasurable turn of events; it's a constant accompaniment to all activities. Joy arises from within each moment of existence, rather than from any other source... The world one sees is illuminated by the exquisite beauty and perfection of creation.

Dr. Hawkins description shows joy as a sacred space, different from worldly happiness. Joy exists solely in the present moment and is not determined by circumstance; happiness on the other hand, comes and goes with the people and events of our lives, and can be manufactured through memories or visualizations of future dreams and goals. Transitioning from happiness to joy requires a deep commitment to spiritual practice; we can all choose to be happy at any given moment; entering a state of joy, however, is immersion into a state of being.

As joy sees through the eyes of the Goddess Lover, it does not reason or think or label; it simply contains the essence of deep appreciation for the whole of life. Joy loves what is—this is also the essence of appreciation.

I AM GRATEFUL FOR...

Growing up, I was taught through school and family to say thank you and to acknowledge the efforts of others. I was not taught the deeper exploration of gratitude as a state of being. I know many people who are outwardly grateful and well mannered yet their hearts are immersed in fears that prevent true moment-by-moment appreciation. For them, appreciation is a single act and often the act expects something in return even if that something is the pride of being a gracious and kind person.

When I stay present to the moment, I notice a tremendous feeling of awe for Life that brings bliss to my senses. When I later record my experiences, trying to capture the essence, I see that it comes simply from my availability to be in open-hearted Now.

The human ego wants to make things complicated so I am not going to tell you "Ten Steps to Gratitude"; in fact I encourage you to not "do" anything at all to embody appreciation, the sacred expression of joy. The secret of the Madonna Code is *Here, Now*. Simply be aware of what it feels like in your body to have present moment appreciation. Notice your body singing through sensations; notice the thoughts that try to take you away and let them gently dissolve as you return to awareness of the feeling state of appreciation. Notice your heart as you gaze at a flower; notice how it swells with love when you are centred simply on the essence of the flower and not the personal meaning you give it. The flower blooms through you, opening your heart as you receive it within. This awareness is what happens when you merge with the present. Again, you need do nothing!

JOURNAL INSIGHTS:
THE ART OF DOING NOTHING

As I read Elizabeth Gilbert's travel memoir Eat, Pray, Love, *I am reminded that many cultures cultivate appreciation by doing "nothing." They take time to rest, eat good food, celebrate, embrace friends and feel intimacy, connection and joy run through their bodies, hearts and souls. North Americans tend to perceive this as doing nothing: they idolize work and minimize the pleasure of the moment. Vacations are okay because they say to themselves, "I deserve this holiday and have worked hard for it!" Daily bouts of "doing nothing" is a threat to their "hard worker" identity that only believes itself worthy if it achieves through massive action. With this identity, joy can never become a reality; the moment by moment appreciation is all but lost.*

ℒOVERS AND ℐOY

When lovers experience joy within themselves it is the greatest gift they bring to their relationship. Through the discovery of the depths of eternal joy the lover naturally and freely offers this to the other; and few people on this earth can resist the authentic joy of another human being. I believe that when people are in love they may be touching the tip of this joy, perhaps for the first time in their lives. They recognize the awesome power and beauty that love contains; they exist in the moment with each other and see the world much like a child in awe of life.

In the movie *Eat, Pray, Love*, Liz (played by Julia Roberts) is about to close the door on a new relationship—one of the first times that she is truly in love. Suddenly, as her world is focused on this lover, their intimacy and the great beauty and joy of their relationship, she resists it, believing she is unbalanced. This is a common reaction for many who discover powerful love, retracting with the reasoning voice rather than listening to the wisdom of the heart. Just a couple of hours before she is to head back to New York from a year long journey of travel and self-discovery, she is offered wisdom that changes the course of her life forever: her teacher, Ketut, tells her that being in love is not being out of balance. Sometimes, the experience of intimate love is exactly what we need to bring us to balance.

This advice is heart wisdom: what appears to be unnatural is the most natural thing in the world. Being in love is part of our organic essence because we naturally express ourselves as joy. Everyone and everything around us suddenly become the love that we are. What is unnatural is to close the heart and close the feeling aspect of our nature. Babies and young children show us that it is natural to feel everything from the heart and to live in a state of wonder. Being in love creates a state of remembrance—that we are unequivocally born in love; through the alchemy of intimacy, we taste a long yearned for, suppressed aspect of our Goddess heart.

JOURNAL INSIGHTS: THE ROOM OF POSSIBILITIES

I am meditating and I see a door. As I press down on the handle I can see that the room inside is filled from ceiling to floor with a bouquet of fresh flowers. As I write about joy and love, feeling into the Divine, I see that each single flower represents a time that I chose to open to love. The room is my Goddess Heart, and each time I open to love, another flower appears, blooming me open to Life. As I write I can feel my soul filled with the flowers of YES. Yes I am loving what is, yes I am in-joy, yes I am the Goddess of Lovers and hold them in my embrace, showing the world what is possible. I want to stay in this room forever...

INDULGING IN JOY ... NOW

The Goddess does not delay joy. She showers herself with radical love, the very waters of life. Cascading over her body, this water is never static; just as joy, in order to be active in her, is never static. Joy comes fully alive with the universal, Divine Feminine flow of life. If we resist this flow and try to stop change from coming in by worrying about the past or having anxiety about our future, then we rob ourselves of our birthright and miss the opportunity to give it to others. Like the harp and the rose, joy gives off one of the highest vibrations on our planet; it is meant to be spread as far and wide as possible. In this respect, joy is a form of prayer, a wordless, powerful energy that emanates from your being to countless others.

In a touching YouTube video, *Bodhisattva in Metro*, a man enters a subway car filled with quiet, solemn, unhappy people and starts to laugh. He laughs quietly at first and then becomes more and more expressive. People begin to smile, and then a few giggle, and soon the entire car is filled with unstoppable laughter. This carries on for a few minutes and then the man who initiated the laughter leaves; the entire car gradually returns to its solemn state. The faces of the passengers reveal the emptiness of their lives, void of joy. It is a powerful reminder that any one of us at anytime can fill a whole stadium with present moment wonder, awe, curiosity, or any one of a host of feelings connected to joy. It is also a reminder that most of us resist joy and do little to nurture its natural state within.

My friend, Kim Tebbutt, does not delay joy. She is the most joyful Goddess I know. Her radiant light is captivating, and everyone notices it. I asked Kim if she would comment on the joy that is within her. She said, "Joy and love are intertwined like lovers. An open heart is the foundation of joy." Kim looks at the beauty around her and says, "I am in awe of everything because everything radiates love. Whether wounded or not, there is love inside all of us at the core. That's what brings me joy. A deep knowing and a deep trusting in that."

Kim says everything is perfect in its imperfection and she trusts in that: "When I stop and I breathe and I look through those 'joy as birthright' eyes of mine, and they start to see the beauty in everything, that's when I go back to a place of trusting and knowing. Looking at everything through the eyes of love, all falls into place and my heart is peaceful again."

Kim believes she was born with joy; that everyone is born with the capacity for joy. She does not have the "easy" life yet like so many courageous and spirited people, she thrives where many do not. She notes, "Some of us have to dig so deep, and I believe we all have it in our heart. Some of us have to dig deeper than we ever imagined."

I asked Kim if she had a spiritual practice that assists in digging deep to see love and become joy. She paused and with her gentle wisdom, replied, "Soften your eyes—to go from fear to love—to see beyond the craziness to the innocence. Accept. Go beyond fear and every emotion that stems from fear, and then go to every emotion that is rooted in love."

Kim says that when a friend was feeling like she could no longer go on with her life, Kim had to remind her of this softening of the eyes. "You have to go deeper than you have ever gone before. Inside of you at the core of your being is love. You find it and you will start to come out of this again." Sometimes we just have to be reminded to excavate until our treasure is no longer buried—to have another witness the truth of our heart.

Kim is an author of children's books focusing on the Divine. She is also writing a thought provoking inspirational book for adults that is one of her tributes to joy. This is a poem she wrote a number of years ago to honor joy:

OUR BIRTHRIGHT ... THE CHILD WITHIN

Delight in the beauty that surrounds us
Listen to the silence, notice the song
A magical musical lyric comes bubbling up from within
Breathe in the effervescent moment
As we remember we are children of God again
Joyfully we start to smile in wonderment
As the beauty of the moment captures us and carries us away
On a rapturous journey, a connection to all that is everywhere
Feel our light radiating out from within
As our God love shimmers up to the surface and beyond
Pure Love
Cast our light out to those around us
Share God's gift to all
Unconditional Love
A gift for each and every one of us
Our Birthright
Sense the presence of every cell
that shares the moment with us
Accept God's Grace in Everything that is.

When the Goddess blooms into love, she feels full. When she closes her heart, there is a subtle and invasive loneliness that settles in; not because of what she doesn't have, but because of what she does have that she has closed the door to. This door, or portal, is the container where love soaks in its own waters of Divine goodness. It is here that you can bring everything that is love and all that is trying to be love, all your hurt and pain, and let it be accepted and nurtured. This is the Madonna Code; this is the essence of joy.

Sacred Practice

♥ When I first presented a chapter of this book to my editor, with whom I have a long-standing relationship, she placed her palms down on my papers, looked me straight in the eyes and asked, "Where is the joy in this writing? What happened to you?" At that time I had concealed much of my private life and was trying to write my book at a safe distance from my heart. It wasn't working. She knew that I was hiding behind scholarly words and abstract ideas. She told me I needed to grieve and then go back and write. The moment I got home, chapter in hand, I collapsed on the bed weeping. I cried for two more weeks and when I was done, my heart began to speak. As best I could, I began to dictate.

♥ Breathe into your deep seated emotion and allow it to run through you; write down all of the ego's beliefs and judgments and assumptions and stories, and as you write, accept the voice and give it full freedom to vent; then destroy the paper, witnessing that the thoughts you just recorded are nothing more than illusion. Now you are ready to discover what your clear heart has to say. When the heart is not covered by hurt and fear, it will speak its joy; what does this joy sound like to you?

♥ While I was in an angel empowerment retreat with Cindy Smith, I carefully scanned the agenda upon arrival and my heart pounded with fear: zip lining through the mountains across a river was not my idea of fun. I am afraid of both heights and speed. To distract myself from this upcoming event and follow instructions for the course, I prepared myself to release a lifelong fear that had inhibited me from living the life of my dreams. I recorded it on a single sheet of paper *and carried it with me as I dangled high in the mountains, whispering to myself, "I can do this." As I zipped across the earth and heavens, feeling the wind on my face and seeing the rushing waters beneath me, I did not just intellectually know I could do anything and be anything—I felt it as part of my very existence. Later that evening we held a ceremony by fire and one by one, watched our fears burn up with the paper. I felt strong inside and my heart was warm. Guidance shared that I was to relax and enjoy life. I focused more on the joy within my body; the miraculous space that was free, wide open and ready to experience the precious moment of being with my courageous sisters.*

❤ *Anytime you want, you can hold your own private ceremony of writing down fears, burning them and feeling the release and the joy that follows. Notice the feelings in your body and stay with this state, here in the moment. Later that day or the next day, be aware of your capacity to see joy in things that you never noticed before. Open to your joy as you open to a lover, with the wonder of a boundless heart.*

ℒOVER OF ℘EACE

David Hawkins' research in muscle testing shows that peace has the highest energetic vibration next to pure God-state, or enlightenment. Peace is the culmination of all the other forms of love. In terms of the Goddess Lover, peace is the ultimate form of freedom in a relationship. When there is no drama or controlling of the other person, needing him or her to be other than what they are, each lover experiences the giving and receiving of radical love. My favorite quote on this topic is by Wayne Dyer: "Love is the ability and willingness to allow those that you care for to be what they choose for themselves without any insistence that they satisfy you."

Peace is this radical love. It doesn't come through sharing the same values and beliefs; it won't appear by searching for qualities that you like and working to change what you don't like. While I never fully reached this state with my husband, particularly during our divorce, I did discover it with my mother. For many years I tried to change her and my rage would build because her way of thinking and acting was so different from mine. I also felt that she was trying to change me. It was only when I stepped into radical heart love that I experienced her as another person on her individual journey rather than the role of mother that I wanted her to live up to.

Peace is compassion, and compassion is surrendering to all of what comes to us as love. With my mother, I did not see the love when I felt my anger. Now, I do not need to wait for circumstances and behaviors and conversations to change in order to see the love and be loving. I can just be with her.

Sacred Practice

💜 *Meditate on the Wayne Dyer quote about love. Where are you holding back from the true expression of love? Lean into the heart-wisdom within and practice surrendering to all that comes to you as love (everything your ego considers to be both unlovable and easily loveable).*

💜 *Inquire into your resistance to self compassion and compassion for others. Are you afraid of losing something or someone if you surrender to compassion? Do you fear betrayal if you make yourself vulnerable? Once you honestly answer these questions, examine the truth of each of these assumptions or beliefs that block compassion. Use Byron Katie's, "The Work", a series of four questions that help you examine the truth of a thought or belief. Katie starts by asking, "Is this true?" and then proceeds to, "Is this really true?"; "Who are you when you believe this is true?"; "Who are you when you believe the opposite is true?" She then asks people to come up with a turnaround statement that would indicate more of the truth that comes from our deepest love—the wisdom of the Goddess Heart.*

SACRED LOVE

Peace and joy are both states that exist in sacred love. In these states, meaning-making is transcended. There is no separation through the mind; no judging, categorizing, or comparing.

The Goddess Heart merges with the Virgin Heart as she places her full awareness on the newness of the moment and the surrendering of any thoughts based on the past or future. There is a complete willingness to enter the state of purity in which love exists—the radical love that knows no fear of loss or rejection.

This state is what I think of when envisioning a pure intimacy, rare as it may be. We bring so much to the table (or to the bed) when we meet for the first time or for the 200th time. By surrendering to the infinite moment where no ego exists; no expectations of happiness, hurts, or betrayals; nothing of what would influence the deeper, soul connection between two people, there is an opportunity to unite fully in Sacred Love.

Byron Katie once said that every touch, look, kiss, everything in a sexual encounter, can have "meaning". But in making it "mean" something—he cares or I need her or he is not paying attention—the drama of our personal story about the relationship increases expectations that our partners must fill a need or make us happy. Without this meaning you open yourself to the full potential of each loving, intimate action, whether it is a kiss, a touch, a conversation, or a sunbeam. Each experience becomes a doorway to connecting to God.

This sacred connection is what keeps romance alive. Romance is a state of being rather than the stuff of fairytales. It is the willingness, discipline at times, to be the Virgin; to be that which is Beginner; each moment a new beginning.

The moment there is a surrendering of "meaning" comes a freedom within the relationship that gives space for Sacred Love to grow, for romance to bloom. This moment fundamentally shifts consciousness. The couple becomes one with the Divine. I believe that conscious couples are showing up more and more to be lightworkers, together healing and creating and encouraging others to join communities that do the same.

SACRED PRACTICE

♥ *Meditate on the topic of romance. How does your experience of romance nurture or close your Goddess Heart? What beliefs do you have about the stages of life or stages of a relationship that cause either an opening of your romantic heart, or a resistance to it?*

♥ *With your partner, plan an evening together in which you focus completely on each other, bringing all of your open heart to each moment. If your attention strays to the past or the future gently bring it back to the present. Experience your partner as though it is the first time you have met; discover through conversation, touch and laughter, the newness, joy and purity of this relationship. Discover Sacred Love.*

JOURNAL INSIGHTS:
THE FOUNDATION OF SACRED ROMANCE

When I look at the shelves of a local bookstore, I am intrigued by the fact that there is no section related to making love but a large section devoted to sex. In fact, the word sex appears on the vast majority of the titles. While I have no issues with books that are marketed with the word sex, I was disappointed that I could not find a single book that contained the word love.

There is a power that is generated in lovemaking that comes deep from within the heart and opens the heart wide and vulnerable and free. There is the feeling that we are indeed God's most beloved creatures and completely and utterly free when we immerse ourselves in making love.

I believe that this power is layered upon a foundation of self love connected to our divinity. When we practice opening our hearts to the vastness of Life, to all there is—without holding back, without repressing, without shrinking back or pushing through—we develop the heart-opening capacity necessary to move from a sexual relationship into a Sacred Romance.

THE GODDESS OF ROMANCE

A Sacred Romance honors the other as an extension of the Divine and remembers self as Divine. This romance is one of true unity where the "we" becomes real, and the "I" becomes the illusion. It is not romance in the sense of what you do for each other. It is romance as an essence, as a state of being. It is heart-centered love that transcends the couple, containing the God-energy that emanates into a room full of people and even entire communities. Think back to a time when you witnessed a couple that had this state of being; where they adored, loved and honored one another and you were aware of their love relationship with others and with Life.

In Sacred Romance, there is an element of constant creation versus stagnation. Because both partners are willing and practice opening to all there is, they begin to create what life and business coaches call "the third entity". That is, their common discipline of opening has merged to create a level of possibilities and experiences not available to one person. This is true both of love making and creating an idea, product or service. The third entity, or what I like to call the "we", is what makes good relationships great. It is the difference between a relationship that merely endures its time on earth and a relationship that blooms open to God.

In my experience, some people have difficulty attracting and keeping a Sacred Romance because they are not committed to living fully with an open heart. Expectations and agendas abound, based on emotional residue of the past. What seems like logical demands—I want a man or woman who is trustworthy and listens to me—often stems from the emotional residue of a past betrayal or loss of confidence. Whenever we set up agendas and expectation, our memories from the past are controlling us, making us slaves to the emotions we experienced then and are recreating now.

At sixteen, I was dating my first love. During this four-year on-again-off-again relationship I felt repeatedly betrayed. Rather than my boyfriend admitting he wanted to end our relationship, he would simply stop calling me, and soon enough, I would see him with another girl. This made no sense to my heart, and at twenty, I left the relationship for good. I was determined that my future boyfriend or husband would not so much as look at another woman and certainly not be in her presence without me! This continued for another decade, lessened with marriage and then heightened dramatically with my divorce. Once again, fear gripped me and when I wanted to enter a new relationship I spent most of my time thinking about how to control potential loss and disappointment. My heart was a fortress, locked up and guarded with the soldiers of my fear.

This fear and corresponding negative emotions can be triggered in an intimate relationship, yet our authentic love feelings are those that come from completely opening our heart to the present moment, with no agenda. For some of us, this is difficult to do because we may be vulnerable and allow our hearts to completely open, becoming one with the bliss of our divinity, yet a short time later attach meaning to this love feeling with unhelpful core beliefs or expectations, like "He should love me more", or "He doesn't listen so he really doesn't care", or "Am I good enough?" These thoughts are linked to emotional patterns of behavior that take making love to making fear—a subconscious fear that convinces us that we are flawed in some fundamental way. This often shows up as blame and anger towards another for not meeting our expectations.

Sacred Practice

The first step in creating love making that is a state, versus a fleeting experience, is to focus on the discipline of loving yourself. The discipline of "making" love or rather, remembering love, within yourself. It is the discipline of remembering who you really are.

♥ *For the purpose of an intimate relationship, this self love can be worked at daily by coming back to pouring love within your heart to all parts of your body in an act of complete present moment surrender to love.*

♥ *When meditating, follow your breath in and out of your body, envisioning it as love coming in and out. This flow of giving and receiving love is critical to the full acceptance of self, coming back to the original truth of who you are.*

♥ *Take time to immerse yourself in a love meditation where your heart's energy expands to fill your body, the room you are in and your entire community. Fill your family, friends and strangers with love. In this expanded state, give love to those you've had conflict with, either now or in the past.*

♥ *Dance in the soft light of love with a candle and music with a melody, rhythm or tone that reflects your deepest heart. I recommend harp music; it has the highest vibrational frequency of any instrument and is the instrument of angels.*

♥ *Listen to chakra clearing music, regularly tuning in and returning to your clear heart, releasing any toxins and emotional debris. The most significant aspect of living with an open heart, where sex really does become love making, is to retain this clear heart that remains open to the present moment of the Divine within you and your partner.*

♥ *Paying attention to your senses and learning to heighten them by focusing on them during the present moment is also critical in enduring love. I used to take for granted the sense of taste in eating, smell in nature and touch when I held a special piece of fabric for a dress I wanted to buy. I never associated this amazing gift with lovemaking. It brings out such deep gratitude for the gift of the other; the gift that they bring to you through your senses.*

Ultimate romantic connection is not born of an idea of what romance is, but rather, is born of the senses, and when bodies feel alive with connection and hearts are open to love with no expectation, then romance is a very real and tangible state. Nurture it as an extension and expression of the love you are.

Too often, as couples get used to being together, they lose intimate connection and part of this is due to less and less attention on the present moment awareness of the senses. Using our intellectual gifts while simultaneously attempting to be in present moment, heart-opening romance tends to produce even more distance. The Wizard Lover, then, is someone who turns off the mind and turns on the heart: mundane moments become magical through the Now.

The Goddess "Certification"

In this chapter, the Goddess heart is centered simply on the opening of the heart as it accepts and loves all that is. Keeping the beautiful simplicity of this in mind, remember that you are certified to love. Whether this is your love for a lover, community, or self, you do not need to be trained to love; by virtue of your birth, you have all the joy, peace, wisdom, passion and energy within. Waiting. Join me now in the journey of the Goddess, as She enters another realm of consciousness: the Heart of the Queen.

Meditative Reflections for the Goddess Heart

- ♥ Every experience is a doorway to my connection with God.

- ♥ I radiate joy from the depths of my Sacred Goddess Heart.

- ♥ I am an alchemist of intimacy and feel deep connection with myself and my beloved.

7

THE HEART OF THE QUEEN: SACRED LEADERSHIP

AMONG MANY OTHER CHILDREN, I grew up with a few images of the good and powerful queen, but the images that remain forever etched in my mind are those of the Ice Queen. In media and fairytales, this queen is cool, distant and even barbaric. It was an image I later observed in newspapers and on TV; I remember hearing about the harshness of the Iron Lady, Margaret Thatcher, and the cool, unfeeling nature of Queen Elizabeth. Patriarchal society has encouraged the belief that a woman in power abandons her feminine side and castrates with her masculine energy. The sacred potential of the queen, however, is the same as that of a king; she is connected to her feminine heart energy and her masculine focus and direction, becoming and inspiring Love in Action.

The Divine Feminine queen is the sacred activist that blends the receptivity and acceptance of the All with the fire of passion for a world that returns to love; to natural justice for all. She is the master of love, and to be a master of love, she both feels love for others and shows it. She sends loving energy to the world and helps our brothers and sisters through time, money, resources and her sacred gifts. She is the Queen of our children's children and beyond; her legacy is that of the shift from a fear-based society to a love-based society.

Just as Jesus was misunderstood when he challenged perceptions of the word "king" and "kingdom", so too has Mary been misunderstood when referred to as "queen". Mary is known around the world as Queen Mother, Queen of Heaven and Queen of the Angels. But she has been overlooked as a woman who lived her life in holy leadership with the courage and strength to inspire a return to love and compassion for all. This type of leadership invites all women to open their feminine heart while activating their masculine, emerging as both the essence of love and love in action.

One of the challenges for women who hear the call to sacred leadership is to merge their Divine Feminine with their masculine energy, co-creating a new world where vast changes take place through an open heart. Many of us have seen and been involved in attempts at monumental positive change and yet we have also witnessed what can happen in the absence of authentic Queen energy. With a closed heart and resistance to what is, there can be no permanent change.

I believe the Divine Feminine in harmony with masculine energy is powerfully represented through the Black Madonna. This image, in both paintings and sculptures around the world, often depicts Mary as a black woman who is connected to the earth and represents unity with nature, the essence of fertility and the earthiness of motherhood. She is also the powerful transcendent spirit who is the great Goddess; she has a direct Divine connection while simultaneously experiencing her humanity and the depths of sorrow. The Black Madonna is an image that more and more women are relating to because this is the Mary that unites, rather than the Mary created by a patriarch that separates and divides. She is the integration of our bodies, minds and souls. Marion Woodman, in *Conscious Femininity*, says that the Black Madonna "is the bridge between the head and the heart". As the masculine mind of ideas and concepts bridges with the feminine heart of radical love, the potential for a new paradigm of leadership emerges. When the Dalai Lama said, "The world will be saved by the western woman," he was referring to the Black Madonna in all of us; the Queen whose time has come.

In Andrew Harvey's stunning book, *The Return of the Mother*, he explores the androgynous nature of Christ, who, through Mary, merges the queen/king within. He urges us to do the same:

Only when we have invited back and reintegrated the sacred feminine with every aspect of our perception and action will we begin to see who Christ really is and has always been—the complete sacred androgyne, the full Son of the Mother-Father...a vision of transcendence and immanence, of Love and service, divine absorption and action, mystical passion and the most total imaginable call for actual transformation here on earth, a transformation of everything that prevents the realization here of the Father-Mother's laws of justice and love.

Recently I attended a workshop in which the topic of feminine and masculine harmony came to my awareness. I recognized the deep peace that comes from fully accepting and uniting my male and female within. I saw that my heart was a key to this unification and harmony because it is the container of loving and accepting the and/both, the All. Yet my ego had developed strong boundaries and expectations around the male and female within. It was as if they had developed personalities, rules and roles that were so habitual and defined by society, experiences and current consciousness, that I became male or female energy at different times; I never experienced the two coming together, as my heart would have me do naturally.

Children who do not yet have a sense of ego identity flow freely between their more masculine or directive, assertive, action-oriented selves to their wide open, expansive receptivity to the All. They navigate the both/and of the heart naturally and with great joy and ease. As adults we have lost this navigation by holding on to what makes us feel safe, powerful and loved, even if that very thing is damaging to us in the long run.

MY PATH TO THE QUEEN WITHIN

Many women I talk to tell of childhood experiences that left them wondering whether it was safe and good and right to be a girl. I too, had these experiences and blocked them from my memory for decades. The stones I threw and the stones thrown back at me confirmed my belief that it was not okay to enter into the wild unpredictability of the feminine. It was not okay to be part of the mystery, the uncontained. My job was to control my life and never again be placed at the mercy of someone else. I stopped being a girl and ordered my feminine heart to leave.

With great determination I entered the adventurous and reliable world of boys. I became a boy in a young girl's body, playing with my brother's friends out on the soccer field, forcing the ball to go my way and usually succeeding. I loved to be goalie and sacrificed my body to ensure no goal was ever scored. While other girls my age got out their dolls and macramé, I got out Star Wars figurines and battled with my guy friends. Life was good and I was happy.

In my teens I became aware of my feminine essence. Being admired and pursued felt good. My identity then became one of an alluring young woman who continued to manage, direct and navigate men to control outcomes. My body and expression had changed. My intent to be a man had not. I could no more receive love than I could freely give it.

I had made friends with a few girls but did not trust them, their emotions, or their fickle nature. They could turn on a dime. At least I knew where a man stood in life. And this assurance was what led me to marriage. My parents were surprised, especially my father, who was certain I would remain single and childless due to my masculine, all-consuming passion for work and achievement.

Dubbed the "wizard of romance" by Marianne Williamson, David Deida says that no matter what, one person in a partnership will take on the primary masculine role and one, the feminine. If a woman is predominantly feminine at her essence, then to shift to the masculine often means the death of genuine attraction and intimacy. I weep now in seeing that I refused to give up my role as male; that I continued to play out this comfortable, strong, safe role with my partner, who by default, reverted to a more feminine role. I was the one who made decisions on where to go, what to do and who to do it with. I was the one who chose where my kids would get their education, how they would be raised and what activities they would join. I did it all. And felt happy doing it.

I wish I could say at what point I recognized the need for my feminine heart. It was not an immediate insight or a single event that changed me. I do know that Divine Chaos, or what looked like all hell breaking loose, occurred when I woke up to a deeper aspect of self. Amongst separation with my husband, my business partners and illness, I found my feminine heart chained up, under lock and key. I heard its whispers, its relentless calling, and began my search to free it from the unbearable weight of the past.

The blessing in Divine Chaos is that it always holds a message for our soul's growth. Sometimes the message shows up through other people; they are the temporary navigators of our souls. Angels in waiting.

For a year, I observed at a distance the journey of one of these angels, Nancy Kerner, and over time had a yearning to learn from her. She encouraged me to be in circle with a group of women. This was a frightening prospect for me: a woman who only trusted herself and, occasionally, God. This experience of being with other women taught me to open to the profound wisdom, love and gifts of the feminine as well as the vulnerability of being open to others and brave the world of self forgiveness. I never again would view women and my relationship with them in the same way. They were warriors of the heart, the ones who stimulated openness; they saw the crack in the concrete of my heart and called it forth to grow into a love embrace that dissolved the walls I had built over four decades. My fortress was no more.

As Divine Guidance would have it, the women in the circle talked about being given spiritual names and later that week I heard a voice from within whisper "Alhambra." I was not familiar with this word but felt that it was my given spiritual name. A few days later I discovered that it is a famous tourist site in Grenada, Spain that was once a fortress and is now considered a palace.

My heart, once a fortress, is now my palace, a place I can welcome all aspects of self and others. It is my place of victory, celebration, mourning, rage, curiosity—all of it. It is the place where I honor my feminine and masculine, giving them space to merge and become part of the unified Source of all love in action.

More recently, I have experienced being almost completely in my feminine heart and yearning for the direction and focus of the masculine to enter my life. Since it had once dominated my way of being, I was familiar with its energy, yet I had immersed myself so much in my feminine that I was seeking direction from outside of me, often at the expense of my own personal power. When I realized the lack of harmony between my female and male, with my female demanding the male within to *act*, I initiated the dance of these divine energies.

SACRED PRACTICE

♥ *Create a loving symbol that represents both your masculine and feminine power as it comes to you from the Divine. Three years ago, a friend called me the lioness and I was shocked because subconsciously, I had always related to the female lion in her feminine and masculine attributes: her motherly nurturing instinct, provider of life through birth and source of food and her ability to work together in community during the hunt with focused clarity and intention. If ego-associated images show up when you are thinking of a symbol, showing you negative things of the masculine and feminine, acknowledge lovingly and allow them to dissolve without struggle.*

♥ *Hold your symbol now in your heart as you breathe in and out from that place. Imagine every detail of this symbol including what it looks like, how it smells, the size of it, the texture, the sound, the feeling. Feel into its feminine and masculine sides; the gifts they bring to your heart.*

♥ *Now bring this symbol deep into the depths of your being, allowing it to be received at the core of your heart to help you navigate challenges and enhance the beauty and flow of Life.*

♥ *Extend the field of grace created by this image beyond your body into the room or space that you are in, and then further beyond into your community and then lastly out into the world beyond.*

♥ *Finish with gratitude to your Source for being a conduit of the grace that shifts the world with every act of love.*

THE SHADOW MASCULINE
AND SHADOW FEMININE

The Shadow side of the human psyche is that which is uncovered or in the dark, longing to be accepted and invited within our hearts. It is the part of us that we don't enjoy seeing in others; we want to judge these habits or ways of thinking in others and find that certain people who possess these traits are a trigger for our negative emotions. I have done much work with my shadow side, contemplating what triggers me and why; I learned to accept shadow parts of me along with the parts that I perceived as "worthy".

Recently I became more aware of specific shadow aspects of my masculine and feminine. As I experienced enormous resistance to either the male of female within, I closed myself to either women or men, depending on what part of myself I was "acting out of". My Shadow Masculine comes out as defensiveness, aggressiveness and exerting control over others. In the last couple of years coming into my Divine Feminine, I resented the Shadow Masculine within and tried to do everything to make it go away, pretend it wasn't there or intellectually tell myself what needed to be done with this monster.

I was blessed with another teacher who, through the experience of feeling into my heart, reminded me to allow this Shadow Land and see it as an observer. This Observer is aware of the thought processes or labeling the mind usually delights in. The Observer simply notices, allowing this to dissolve without assistance from any part of me that might feel the need to fix it. Rather than buying into the illusion that this Shadow Masculine defines who I am, I see it is an aspect of me that tries to be helpful in its own way.

When my Shadow Feminine appears she is completely run by emotional residue of the past and is triggered by situations that occurred many years ago. Addicted to the drama of the moment, she takes on everyone's negative emotions and becomes absorbed in the worries of the world. I thought it would work to close my heart to the Shadow Feminine, reasoning that it simply would not show up if I did that. I was wrong. The more I resisted, the stronger the reactions became.

I have found that guilt, or the Good Girl/Bad Girl syndrome rears its head when I indulge the Shadow Feminine. Rather than accepting and loving her I go to a place of shame and guilt for being that which I "know better" not to be. My mind says, "For God's sake, you are in your forties! You should have this one figured out by now!"

Media loves the Good Girl/Bad Girl archetypes and plays on these constantly to get people to buy their magazines and watch their shows. Almost a decade after Brad Pitt's alleged affair, Jennifer Aniston is the Angel and Angelina Jolie is the Devil. And why can't Brittany Spears be more like Carrie Underwood anyways? This adoration and build up of the Angel versus the Whore or the Pure versus the Twisted is actually a commentary on our deep-seated beliefs that women must behave in a particular way in order to be valued or avoid being shunned.

Also fascinating is that many of these female stars have difficulty retaining their own feminine, closing their hearts in an effort to protect themselves. Old photos of some of the top stars reveal a naturalness of opening and wonder and joy. Over time, their image shifts as they meet the demands of the media's version of sexy woman, while simultaneously being told to move, sing, act...like men. This shift to please the world around them brings them to various forms of addiction; they have the "to die for" body, while their spirit slowly dies within.

Dancing in harmony with the masculine and feminine within is uncharted territory for me, for movie stars and for most people I know. Our consciousness is only now beginning to touch on the possibility of uniting these two life forces and even now, there is much hatred and distrust for aspects of the feminine or masculine in many parts of the world. In some countries the resistance has been geared more to the Shadow Male, abusing it rather than working with it to create harmony. Our prisons are filled with Shadow Masculine; misunderstood and misguided, our men are left abandoned and rejected.

When we cry for help, when we hit rock bottom, our only hope of completely opening is to accept both the feminine and masculine aspects of self and to love them equally, holding the space for them to co-exist. When we close our hearts to receive love and give compassion or when we procrastinate with the purpose we've been given, our destiny has no chance of being fulfilled. It is a managed life instead of a life magnified by the great inherent beauty of the masculine and feminine.

I'm not suggesting an equal distribution of male/female energy or that one ought to be as much in their feminine energy as their masculine. Everyone will have their own felt sense of what is their natural balance and that changes multiple times in a lifetime. Suggesting a ratio puts this beautiful synergy of energies into an intellectual pursuit with a "right" answer or a single key to happiness. This energy of One is much like being part of a dance where you are your partner; you are leading self and you are following self; you are giving and receiving love, respect, guidance.

A couple of years ago I listened to an interview with a blind professional ballroom dancer who was asked how he knows when to turn with his leading lady and how to remain on the dance floor without mishaps. He replied that he is so in tune with his partner's body that he feels her tense when she gets close to the outskirts of the floor and gages the degree of that tension to know when to turn or when to move forward or back. This is much like our dance within; feeling exquisitely the moment at which our feminine or masculine divinity directs us and guides us to fulfill our destiny; to dance the dance of our lives.

I believe that the day has arrived that we acknowledge and accept fully the male and female within each of us and that the dance of the male and female within does indeed contribute to the shift in consciousness on our planet right now. It is not only contributing, it creates a different world. When the Divine Feminine energy unites with the Divine Masculine, creation is so powerful, so heart based and harmonious, that it shifts the world's present condition. The Renaissance Man trusts in his inner female whose wisdom of the heart and receptivity to life provide the foundation for his active and directive energy to create. Women today are learning to unite their receptive feminine energy with a male energy that supports, guides and acts to bring their intentions into form.

Sacred Practice

♥ *Create a collage that visually represents your masculine and feminine in harmony. Find photographs and magazine images that inspire co-creation and true leadership of the Queen/King.*

♥ *Ask the female and male images, one by one, if they have something to say to you. Add this message to the collage or find a picture that represents this message.*

♥ *Continue to speak to your male and female essence and when either feels as though they are overtaking the other or becoming the shadow side, stay in communication with them through the images in the collage and through your daily meditation. Ask your female what is it that she needs to receive at this time of challenge and ask your male how he can help her to receive this (action oriented). If your male is becoming too dominant, ask him what he wants and how your female can focus on being receptive and supportive during the action of following through.*

Although I encourage you to be aware of the feminine and masculine aspects within you, there comes a time when duality disappears. In spiritual leadership, there is no existence of opposites. If we truly embrace both the Divine Feminine and Divine Masculine within, we are no longer aware of the two being separate parts of our being—all becomes One. Or perhaps, more accurately, our ego records the essence of feminine and is aware of its masculine traits, but as consciousness elevates, the two dance so intimately that one cannot exist without the other. They become the flame of Eternal Love. The Madonna Code invites you to enter this flame and unveil the Queen within. The world is waiting.

MEDITATIVE REFLECTIONS
FOR THE QUEEN HEART

♥ I dance in the balanced and radiant energy of the Divine Feminine and Divine Masculine within.

♥ I embrace all parts of me in complete acceptance and love.

♥ My Queen Heart is in service to all of Life; I am Love-in-Action.

8

From Princess to Queen: A Journey into the Heart of Community

As a girl growing up in the seventies, I remember watching Disney movies and reading fairytales about young women who battled all odds to get to their prized destination. They were courageous and spirited, yet I dreaded the inevitable romance they would experience because it always led to the same result; individuality melted away as they were rescued by the prince, married him and lived happily ever after as "the wife". I have no recollection of seeing a Princess become a Queen. My assumption was that the Princess is always provided for; her fate is safe in the actions and thoughts of her White Knight. She is happily silenced into the fairytale moment and slips out of her power to lead self and others. She does good deeds to support her man and contributes to the patriarchal values that keep her limited and contained.

The Queen shares her gifts with family and community while remaining in her own power. She neither rescues nor needs to be rescued. She has transcended the victim stories of the Princess and reclaimed her spirit. This reclaiming allows her to stand as a beacon of light for her people—a power centre of love that unites the world with equality and intimacy. As Master Rebirther and community-builder Mahara Brenna says, she leads with, not over; she sees the circle, not the triangle of the patriarchy where one leader rules from above.

Princess Diana's life is an example of the archetypal journey from Princess to Queen. Diana was rescued by a much older prince and in her innocence, played out the quiet, understated role of the princess as expected. After years of dealing with rejection from her new family and from her husband, she emerges as a queen who moves beyond the victim into a woman who was a champion of a just world, a world of compassion, caring and service to others. Diana raised awareness of atrocities across the globe and used her status as princess to embody the Queen, embracing her community with radical and relentless love. As she opened the heart center of England, the collective consciousness of the country shifted. Fondly referred to as, "the People's Princess", Diana ignited the hearts of women everywhere, who yearned to express themselves fully and courageously.

In some ways, the story of Mary parallels this modern day story of a princess. Mary, too, was very young when she took on the role of both mother and wife. She was told at this tender age that her life would not be easy; that she would see great suffering of her child as he grew into a man; and that ultimately, society would reject him. Knowing this in advance would cause the average Princess to be thrown into anxiety attacks while waiting to be rescued by anyone willing to listen. Yet Mary chose to reach within her spirit and call upon her Divine Feminine strength to unite the people, rather than remain separate from them; she chose to be a Healer, to be the people's Queen rather than the archetypal Princess, and even now in reported visitations around the world she continues to be the all embracing, compassionate force of radical love.

In my own life, I have spent much of my journey as a Princess and reveled in the stories and drama that proved why I was separate and alone—stories that showed me that I deserved to be rejected. Yet in my more recent journey as a Queen, I am discovering that true leadership is not about separation, specialness and competition; true leadership is about unity consciousness; it is about knowing and acting in a way that brings people together through the heart of love, rather than dividing through the patriarchal mind.

When I began immersing myself in the Divine Feminine, I had a clear vision of thousands of Marys—all shapes, sizes, skin colors and cultures, walking one by one, slowly making their way to a meeting area. I was surrounded by all of them as I began to speak at an outdoor stage that looked as if the earth itself had conceived it. The image called me to work with women around the world. A couple of years later, I understood that the vision was also a calling to invite all women to be leaders—to reclaim our power.

I believe that women who live the Madonna Code will build community that honors and ignites the Divine Feminine. This movement has already started, at a grassroots level, where small groups of women gather together in circle to heal, create, reclaim and remember. As these groups impact women and give them space to transform, more and more leaders will hear their calling to create what at one time had been a natural part of society: communities of women sharing their love, guiding each other in the ways of the heart and receiving intuitive insights that are nurtured and supported with such a devotion and commitment that every woman recognizes her leadership, the heart of the Queen within.

WOMEN'S CIRCLES

In circle, each woman is equal and each woman is heard. Each woman is welcomed, accepted, loved. It is the heart of the Queen that understands the vital need for women to experience this. Many women are guided to join or create a circle yet may be afraid because they only experience a model of communication and leadership where one person has power over the others, knows better and imparts truth and wisdom (which you have never had access to). It is "the expert" model that closes the heart and simply engages the mind; it is a model that suppresses the true and tender heart of woman and discounts her feminine intuition and ability to invite and inspire intimacy and soul connection.

The model of the expert cannot function within a Sacred Feminine circle since all the women are invited into their deepest wisdom and guidance. When I felt that I didn't know enough to lead a group of women through a journey into their hearts, Anne Marie Wright, a Divine Feminine facilitator throughout Europe and North America, replied, "The only time anyone is ever an expert is in this moment. Can you be the expert in this moment?" I realized then that I was using my ego to discount my part in the circle, to create an identity around what an expert is and how she behaves. I was also not trusting that every woman is every other woman's teacher; true community learns from one another and shares wisdom without pushing it away or feeling the need to judge it.

In conversation with circle mentor Nancy Kerner, I learned that many women are afraid to join or facilitate a circle because of life experiences that equate leadership with an abuse of power. She gives her own experience as an example:

> If I didn't conform I was punished in some way, which included being yelled at, whipped, hit, spanked, neglected and often forgotten. Having four brothers and several fathers while growing up, I was surrounded by men, and then I ended up working in construction where I met my husband at the age of nineteen. What I learned was that when something doesn't fit in the alpha male's world, it will be forced and projected onto you. If I didn't do what they said, they had power over me to keep me from bringing my voice. Force and power over women keeps her contained and under control. Under these circumstances, we are taught that we are stupid and that we don't know what we feel. We are held hostage from tapping into and trusting, our own inner power.

Through these experiences, we don't trust ourselves, and because we cannot trust ourselves, we cannot trust other women. This is one of the reasons for resistance to being in a community of women and for not listening to Divine Feminine Consciousness, the part of her that speaks to her in a feminine tone.

Sacred Practice

Reflect on your feelings about being in a community of women, or in circle with women. Write down any fears or resistance you have. Feel into your body to discover where that uneasiness lives. Is it in your stomach; the center of self-esteem? Is it in your throat, the area of speaking your truth? Go to that area now and ask what it needs from you in order to feel safe, supported and loved. Write these needs down. Visualize the person within who feels this way; is she a child, teenager, mother, daughter, friend? See yourself bringing her to your heart. Give her everything she asks for, from the radical love of your Mother Heart. Imbue her with the white and golden light of protection and divinity and the pink and green light of pure love and healing. See her now as totally safe and supported in entering a community of women, fully sharing her gifts and fully receiving all that the group brings to her in complete love.

Being part of two of Nancy's circles, I witnessed my own voice emerge from the sadness and loss; felt my courage to dream again; to believe in myself through the love and support of the women in circle and our shared experience of the Divine Feminine. I knew that my Queen Heart, the heart of true leadership, was surfacing after years of suppression and denial of my inner truth. Wisdom of the feminine naturally flowed back into my body as I trusted in myself, my intuition and the women around me.

I asked Nancy about the transformation that she is witness to when women join and facilitate circles. With two decades of experience in seeing the return of inner leadership and feminine power through circle, Nancy passionately advocates the benefits of circles:

Vital women's wisdom guides us when we gather in circles to learn about love and how to nurture ourselves and the women around us. Being in a circle of loving, healthy women teaches us how to trust ourselves, our feelings, our emotional inner guidance, and how to listen to our body's wisdom. We discover the many aspects of our intuition as we listen to our inner feminine voice, and how she speaks to us through our dreams, cycles and rhythms of the moon, tides and menses. After menses, we begin a new journey of a constant flow of intuition that opens us to a whole new realm of change called menopause, or 'a pause from the men'. This is where we re-seed our communities of women with wisdom, strength and hope of infinite possibilities. We now teach what we learned and we find ourselves confident in who we are and our power in the world around us.

We understand the importance of being able to ask for help and to receive love in the midst of our pain and vulnerability. More importantly we learn how to heal our past pain and to open our hearts to love again. This love is infinite and abundant when our heart is open. This is why we enter into a circle of women; to find and to share love, creativity, purpose and passion while learning how to have more joy and fun in life. This isn't something that is explained, but it's an experience to be shared through our connection with one another.

Nancy shares her own experience of this:

As an addict in early recovery, there was so much pain in some of the circles and I wanted to transmute the pain into love, yet, I was surrounded by intense alpha male energy in the form of anger. My own mother was like a warrior in survival mode and she was not in a place to receive me and my newfound vulnerability. She simply did the best she could, while coping with her own painful past, and so we were both missing the gentle mothering that healthy women give to one another. I found a sponsor who had this love and nurturing for me and it changed my life. She gave me permission to heal my past wounds.

For the past twenty years leading circles and retreats, I see women become radiant and leave uplifted with a smile, saying, "I feel alive for the first time in my life and you've given me permission to be a woman." Many women are told what is bad, wrong, or negative about us because people misunderstand the power of a healthy woman. The circle opens our hearts and we transcend our egos for a while and dance in the joy of the life force within and around us.

JOURNAL INSIGHTS:
THE JOY OF RECEIVING WHO I AM

As I typed Nancy's last words on my computer I suddenly received a ringing in my left ear then a pressure change and a minute later another ringing—I knew from past experience that guidance was coming through. I listened intently and heard the word "radiance"; I stopped writing to follow the feeling of this word. What happened next was a state of pure bliss in which I felt the presence of joy. It wanted nothing and needed nothing. It was a state that has been rare in my life but as I experience more giving and receiving of the glory of love—through women's circles and through the spiritual practice of loving myself open to the world—I know that I am this state. It is not accessed outside of me but is part of who I am. As I was in this beautiful presence, I heard the voice "I AM." I understood that there was nothing more to do than to receive who I am. Simple, beautiful and awe inspiring: receive who I am.

I felt my heart open like a flower and extend beyond my body, and the joy of this heart opening lifted all the fears and weight of daily concerns from my body. I felt all parts of my body open up. This experience encourages me to come back to joy every day. What am I waiting for? What beliefs do I have that says my reality is the daily challenges of life?" I have a small poster in my bathroom that a friend gave me, and it says, "Good morning. This is God. I will be handling all of your problems today. I will not need your help, so have a miraculous day." I smile every time I read this and know it as my truth. For too many years I have allowed my glory and my gratitude for the Divine to be subdued by pain and worry. It's time to transform that. Being in community with women and gathering a community of women is a way home to the bliss that is our birthright.

When we can tap into this bliss daily; when we meet regularly with other women and open our hearts to the miracles around us and those yet to be created through us, we claim our Queen Heart within. We lead other women, invite them to experience a world beyond their daily existence. We are the igniters of the soul; the harbingers of light that encourage the leader within to live beyond a managed life to the bliss-ings of the magnified life. We bring women back from the dis-ease in their bodies and minds so that they can fulfill their purpose and destiny as conduits of the call to love. Nancy says, "Look around at medical systems, financial systems—all delusions we've created that tell us what our body needs and how to treat it. I'm passionate about the feminine coming back to be the herbalist—we won't need psychiatrists to give antidepressants when we connect to each other through the love of women."

CREATING A WOMEN'S CIRCLE

My journey in leading circles has just begun and my two mentors in this area help me understand the container in which love, safety and personal transformation can occur. They teach me what helps women feel safe to be who they are and open to the experience of the Divine Feminine and their sacred power. Nancy Kerner and Jonina Kirton have decades of experience in facilitating circles. In interview with both of these women, they reveal practical steps in preparing to hold a women's circle. Nancy offers some initial considerations:

> If you want to create a women's circle, be aligned with your vision for it: what kind of topics will you introduce, who are the women you'd like to attract, and what intentions would you like to create for yourself and for the women in the group. Also, prepare women to come with an open mind and heart. It's important to interview the women to make sure that this is the right circle for them, and if not, perhaps suggest another one for them. You can do this with a few simple questions.

Ask them to tap into their body and to share what they are feeling because up until now, no one may have asked them this question. In circle, watch for all the different ways intuition moves through their bodies so they can be aware of what's going on at any given moment. It's totally about being conscious and aware of energy. What do you feel, hear, smell, envision, or sense happening within and around you? The more conscious you are, the more of your intuition you'll be able to access.

Jonina also emphasizes the importance of the body as women enter sacred circle:

A sacred circle is very experiential; you need to bring the body along. As the facilitator you set the tone, hold the space and offer the invitation to the sacred. Opening prayers, cleansing, or clearing and grounding are all rituals that one can use to open the circle, invite Spirit in, and assist the women in becoming more present. So when you start circle you are there, in your body, totally present.

My dance with the divine began as a solitary journey. There was the occasional satsang, the call and response chants and co-ed meditation/discussion groups, but it was not until I entered sacred circles with women that I truly found my authentic voice and experienced the body wisdom that ritual provides. In circle, I found that there is a spaciousness that women intuitively understand. Women's bodies facilitate this knowingness. Each woman has access to it; after all, their body can hold another body, allow it to float. Their body expands, makes room for another. It is in this spaciousness, natural to women, that the heart wisdom lives.

interior

there are no maps for the floating you must do

to get a sense of the whole of yourself

as complex as any map you have ever seen

is the inside of your heart

Jonina Kirton

HEART WISDOM FOR THE QUEEN

As Jonina and Nancy talk about the body and heart, I am aware that I have long neglected ninety percent of my body in favor of one part: the brain. Women's circles allow us to make the journey from the head to the heart and come to a healthy balance of the two within our communities. My former role models of Queen Leadership were those women who were highly intelligent and used their intellect to lead yet never tapped into heart and body wisdom. After meeting Nancy and Jonina and many other women in the community I am now a part of, I understand experientially that circles ignite the harmony of head and heart, providing space for Divine Leadership to emerge.

Nancy shows how simple rituals both within circle and at home can bring this harmony back into our lives:

> We find that by sitting in circles with women and having rituals we can access our heart and the source of our power very quickly. My first ritual came to me from Louise Hay in 1988. Sit with a picture of your inner child and tell her you love her because she was abandoned a long time ago. Get her and hold her hand and say come with me, you're safe now. Look at

yourself in the mirror and tell the inner child within you that you love her. Then tell her you'll take care of her. I sobbed when I did this. No one had spoken to me like that before.

Light a candle—it's a ritual. If I'm in a circle or teleseminar call I light a candle. I like to take a breath—inhale through nose and exhale through mouth—this brings me from head to heart, bringing me into my body. This is the beginning point—the power begins within my heart—the center of my body, center of the Universe. And when I can feel my body, my ego is taking a little nap. I'm grateful that my ego helps me get things done, and my heart allows me to be with the presence of the Divine Feminine. And these rituals that we create in circles for women are designed to be a dance between intellect and heart.

I believe that my experience of travelling with altars in my suitcase across North America and Hawaii taught me that I can create a ritual anywhere I go. I longed for the gentleness of a mother to stroke my hair softly, to hold my hand, to tell me to believe that dreams are possible, and that I have power to manifest these dreams from a thought. So, I thought, if I had these desires, then who else does? If I have a desire to commune with the Divine, who else does? What I found was that we have really neglected the heart—what matters now is that we open the door; arms wide open looking up to the heavens and say, "I surrender to the Divine within me and I see Her in you." Connecting to the presence and energy of the Eternal Mother within you is the most powerful thing we can do as women. I Am She and She is Me.

Sacred Practice

If you are thinking of planning or joining a women's circle, write down your vision for the circle, and see, hear, feel and know the essence of this circle. Reread the suggestions from Nancy and Jonina and use the rituals and practices that are intuitively right for you and the women that you are in community with. Have a discussion with these women about your vision and how they can be part of it. As much as possible, invite all participants of your circle to engage in this process and feel the power of co-creation. When I began to let go of fears that I had to plan and create everything on my own, I discovered that the energy and enthusiasm of a group propels it to heights that could never be reached through the efforts of one person. This is the power of Divine Feminine Leadership as a co-creative and shared experience.

Spiritual Community

As well as gathering in circle, women are opening to the possibility of spiritual companions as a form of community. As women trust their intuition and open their heart to the Virgin and Goddess energy, the radical heart of the Mother and the powerful essence of the Queen's Divine Leadership, they need to share deep, transparent, heart-based conversation that is both received by another and mirrored back; this soul connection ignites our divine essence and brings us powerfully back to who we are as the Divine Feminine.

In *Entering the Castle: An Inner Path To God and Your Soul,* Caroline Myss describes the importance of having such a companion: "Your soul requires both solitary time for prayer and companions of the soul. You need community around you and with you because, as your interior world becomes more alive, you will want to be with people who understand the journey—not your journey, but the soul's journey."

Myss goes on to explain the function of a soul companion:

> A soul companion is not a soul mate but a person with whom you share a bond of reverence for the spiritual journey you are both on and for how you have chosen to walk on this Earth. Soul companions discuss topics that nourish each other's spirits and help each other appreciate the divine gifts in their lives including building friendship networks that support each other's creativity and work in the world. Soul companions use their inner light to illuminate the light in each other. You utilize the gifts of your soul to bring as much truth and wisdom into each other's lives as possible. You are spiritual mirrors for each other, witnesses to each other's sacred experiences.

These spiritual companions are a constant source of inspiration and grounding in my life, as I am reminded to be in this world and not of it. One powerful and practical way to frequently connect with these companions is through a blog. My spiritual writing group shares their journey and each of us has found at least one other person in the group with whom we have co-created a soul connection. This intimacy is built over time, often through meeting in person and through phone calls, and most frequently through blogging. Some of these companions share with me their insights that come amidst adversity and ask for support, just as I do of them.

If you cannot meet in person regularly, which seems to be the challenge for many women, a blog is a wonderful way to connect. Jonina Kirton is one of my spiritual companions, and we share great wisdom and understanding through our writing. Here is one example of a blog she wrote in response to my shock over an ongoing need to control and a refusal to surrender, even in the face of commitment to my spiritual journey:

> I always say, "Hang on to your hat" if you are going to invite Spirit in and decide to live a spiritual life. A lot of what you hold dear will dissolve or transform, in one way or another. This is most true in the area of how we see ourselves. We may be surprised to find that we are not kind or easy going—that we in fact do try to control everything, which is neither kind nor easygoing. We become controlling because we do not trust the universe or anybody in it, including ourselves. We hope to avoid pain and of course this does not work but we keep trying anyway.
>
> A spiritual life requires deep surrender to what is and we do not need to do this alone. Prayer, meditation, chanting, and contemplation will ease us into this surrender. Any pain we feel around all that is blown up, dissolved, or transformed is soothed by these very same practices. Whenever I came to the place where I felt I could not go on I would crank up the chanting music and chant until the fear passed and the pain was transformed into peace, joy, and love for whoever was involved.

Jonina's words provide a source of soothing reassurance to be gentle with my own humanity, and yet a spiritual companion does something else: she does not feed on the victim story nor does she try to save us; she simply is a source of love that shares another perspective, a practical tool, or a warm and receptive heart. She contains the light that we know is within us as well; sharing challenges with a spiritual companion is a deep form of trust and prayer.

JOURNAL INSIGHTS: HOLDING HER IN OUR ARMS

This past month I have listened to my dear friends go through some difficult times; very challenging times indeed. Cancer, separation, suicide, betrayal and loss of a child…it makes me weep to feel the intense pain of my sisters and what they endure as part of their journey, as part of the collective journey.

One thing that is becoming more apparent throughout the years is this mystical bond between women that creates miracles when the women are open. When hearts are open to trust, to have faith in each other, to know, as Nancy Kerner says, "I am She and She is Me." To feel into everywoman and tell her:

IT'S NOT YOUR FAULT.

Rock her, hold her, sing to her, cry with her and help her to remember the all-powerful woman and spiritual being within.

It is our responsibility to hold our sisters in compassion, not competition, hold them in the light that they are, so that when they are ready to find the door, the path will be lit, and they will walk through.

The Sacred Leadership that is coming to this earth is no longer about being on top; being the one in control; being the wisdom that imparts from on high. Leadership now is coming to us as the feminine circle of equality, intuition, compassion and justice for all. It calls for each of us to stand in our power and participate in a new inclusive paradigm. This dream is becoming reality as more women welcome soul sisters to reclaim their open heart and divine self, feeling the unity that is their deepest truth and knowing.

MEDITATIVE REFLECTIONS FOR THE QUEEN HEART

💛 The Eternal Mother sits in circle with me, in me, Now.

💛 I lead from love and in love.

💛 I serve my community in the spirit of unity. All is One.

Afterword: The Call

"We must know that we have been created for greater things, not just to be a number in the world, not just to go for diplomas and degrees, this work and that work. We have been created in order to love and be loved."

Mother Teresa

WHEN ALL OF LIFE IS STRIPPED of egoic concerns there is a pure simplicity that readily reveals truth. The truth of the Madonna Code is the very message of beloved Mother Teresa. For years I labored to discover what my purpose in the world was and how I was to contribute meaningfully to society. One Divine discussion in my most desperate hour cleared all my confusion and I saw what my calling was. Actually, I heard it. With a childlike demanding, I asked Mary to tell me what my purpose in life is. She whispered, "To give and receive love." I didn't understand the profound gift of this response so I asked again, hoping for more details, more personal direction so that I could happily begin fulfilling my destiny. She whispered again: to give and receive love. Relentlessly, I probed for more information, and tirelessly, she gave me the same loving words. It was not until much later that I came to know this message through experience and then by writing about the experience; this book is a tribute to her message.

In being a portal for Divine Love, we are here to answer the greater call to bring our world together in harmony and do all that we can to stop forms of separation that take us away from our Virgin Heart; that isolate us from the radical love of the Mother heart; that keep us afraid of our own Goddess power; that contain us in an old paradigm of leadership where the heart of the Queen is reserved for a special few. Embracing all four Hearts is the essence of the Madonna Code and it is one form of unification that will at last harmonize all that was once divisive: the Feminine and Masculine, the body and the spirit, sex and the sacred, earth and heaven. All join together as one and are equally precious parts of the All, of the great Eternal Love.

Mary is said to have left the earthly plain with body intact: this is referred to as the Assumption. This act, when looked at symbolically, is highly significant to the Sacred Feminine as unifier of all things: Mary shows us the possibility of a world that is not separate, the possibility that heaven is on earth, that we are simultaneously form and spirit. Mary imbued her world with radiant light and showed us that we never have and never will be separate from the sacred heart of the All.

One of the great calls is to integrate all into one and become the love that we are. This requires not only our being state, our receptive chalice. We are called to be both love and love-in-action. We are called to implement change from our sacred chalice so that this change is imbued with the heart of love rather than the egoic fears that halt necessary change and create discord amongst one another. If we hold divinely guided ideas in our hearts, pray for ideas to be carried out in the spirit of the Sacred Feminine and be vigilant in our own leadership role within this process, we all have a chance to change the course of history. The Dalai Lama has called this type of process "compassion": it involves more than a feeling of love; genuine compassion is also the will to assist those who suffer.

It is astounding that Mary has been depicted as a docile and passive woman, when in reality, a closer look at both the woman on earth and the Divine Being in apparitions shows someone who acts courageously in the face of terror. She continued Christ's message after watching her son die in agony and reached such a level of light and love that she was able to ascend with her body intact. As a deity, Mary pleads with humanity to be compassionate and take care of the earth and her children. The Black Madonna image reminds us that her suffering was as real as the suffering we have experienced in our lives and gives us hope that we can all transcend this suffering to be love-in-action, to be of service, instead of becoming inwardly consumed with our own misery.

A final point about Mary is that by being the Pregnant Virgin, she has shown us the ultimate unity of the matriarch and the patriarch. She represents the possibility of the Divine Feminine and Divine Masculine coming together to complete the call of love-in-action. By birthing Christ, Mary Consciousness and Christ Consciousness merge into one powerful expression of the potential within all of us: to be fully in both our humanity and divinity, surrounded by the radical heart of love.

In *The Return of the Mother*, Andrew Harvey makes a passionate plea for a new paradigm that goes beyond history's initial matriarchal rule and the extensive and destructive patriarchal rule that is only now beginning to crumble. He sees that a third movement must take place in order to save our earth from vast and devastating destruction—the sacred marriage:

> Not only should we invoke the sacred feminine, restore the sacred feminine, but this union between the matriarchal and the patriarchal, the sacred marriage, must be accomplished in the spirit of the sacred feminine for it to be real, effective, rich and fecund. It must occur in her spirit of unconditional love, in her spirit of tolerance, forgiveness, all-embracing and all-harmonizing balance, and not, in any sense, involve a swing in the other direction... If we are to really take seriously the journey into the sacred feminine, we must open ourselves to the outrageous truths that are contained in the power of the sacred feminine, the madness of divine love, the wisdom beyond all concepts and categories. The outrageous truth of a flexibility that is paradoxical in its very nature; the truth of a force that can never be talked about but has to be embraced, has to be learned and embodied.

In this book, there are many ways in which to experience the embodiment of the Sacred Feminine. I encourage you to review and renew your commitment to your call by completing the sacred practice actions in each chapter and by nurturing your spiritual practice. A deep and passionate love for your connection to the Divine will assist you in following through with your commitment to a spirit-led life. Nurture yourself by stepping out of isolation to be with a group of women in circle. This too is a transformational and enlightening path to embodying the

Sacred Feminine. Another way to embrace and live the Code is to participate in a retreat. We offer several different retreats and circles that focus on each of the four Hearts of the Madonna; please visit *www.DivineYou.ca* for further information. There are also many helpful free resources on this site, including recorded interviews with several of the facilitators mentioned in this book.

Mary helped me to understand that Sacred Leadership is love-in-action. In meditation, I heard her say, "There is no leadership other than love; the hardship of love becomes the bliss of love when all things are equally loved." Mother Teresa, as a Sacred Activist, understood this radical statement and lived it daily. She once shared this great spiritual paradox: "If I love until it hurts, then there is no hurt, but only more love." We are being called to open our hearts to this radical love that is the essence of the sacred activist.

Love-in-action can support the revival of Mother Earth, compassion for your neighbor, or commitment to a cause; it may also involve regular time in prayer and meditation, to help those that most need our help. This love is found in small acts of kindness as often as it is found in large projects. Where the sacred is, you will find no labels and definitions such as "small" and "large"; no act of service is insignificant, and one is not better than the other. What is important is to come from a simple heart where service is not muddled with identity or ego. A pure open heart filled with the sacred and ready to be of service will do more to change the world than a thousand intellectuals' egos ruminating on ways to save the earth.

This is the time where we are called to go one step beyond our adoration of avatars and angels and activate our own potential to be the light and love that is our essence. We can no longer afford to be distant from the Divine within by seeing ourselves in any way shape or form as less than, different, or flawed. This is apparent in Andrew Harvey's book, *Mary's Vineyard: Daily Meditations, Readings, and Revelations*. Harvey quotes Mary, who, in 1966 in San Damiano, appeared as an apparition with a stunning message:

"You think that I am beautiful? I am beautiful because I love. Do not imagine that your mother is more blessed than you. All who live in Love are blessed as I."

In writing this book, my hope is that you will experience and deeply know yourself as the bridge between humanity and divinity. We are the hands, mouth, feet of love. You may have noticed that the front cover contains my image. This took great courage on my part, yet I felt to live this radical Mary message, we need to explore all parts of who we are rather than looking externally; to enter the Mary in our hearts rather than the Mary created through the perspective of another. I have no doubt that our greatest joy and blessing is to be the conduit of miracles that will elevate and lift humanity to its Divine essence. To be the simple heart that sees the unity of love.

Maintain this simple heart daily by bringing your awareness to the four Mary Hearts within. Feel the essence of the Virgin, the Mother, the Goddess and the Queen. Within the depths of your body, feel the Divine Feminine fill you with radiant, radical, outrageous love. She whispers to you now, "Remember who you are. Your story is my story. Your love, your deepest regret, your passion, your gifts, are mine as well. Remember who you are."

"These are the times of the great return. Yes, after the time of the great suffering, there will be the time of the great rebirth, and all will blossom again. Humanity will again be a new garden of life and of beauty."

Our Lady, Medjugorge, 1986
(as quoted in *Mary's Vineyard*)

The Madonna Code Resources

We offer many free resources to extend and enrich your experience of the practices in this book. Please go to *www.DivineYou.ca* to claim your free gifts and to receive updates on Karen McGregor's retreats, women's circles and conferences.

To have Karen speak at your conference or hold a retreat in your area, please contact: *Karen@DivineYou.ca*

Other Recommended Resources

Women's Circle Mentoring

Nancy Kerner lives her passion of bringing together, in circles and communities, women who want to reconnect with the Source of Her Feminine Power. She is teaching, writing and co-creating Pleasure in Paradise Retreats in Hawaii: *www.nancykerner.com*

Sacred Circles

Jonina Kirton is a Métis/Icelandic poet/author, a mystic and a mother. Her interest in spirituality, writing, facilitation and women's issues has coalesced in her work with sacred circles for women. Look for her at *www.sacredcirclesbook.com*.

Intuition Development

Hannelore, M.S.C., M.S.H. is an International speaker, author, counselor, teacher and Spiritual Life coach offering public and corporate workshops worldwide. She teaches an extensive training program "The Power of Intuition" and facilitates exclusive residential "Communing with Dolphins" retreats in Hawaii and Wilderness Retreats in magical places: *www.Hannelore.ca, www.CommuningWithDolphins.com*

Cindy Smith, developer and teacher of the "Angel Empowerment Certification™ Course" and "Connect to Your Own Power Workshop", is the author of Wings of Love Empowerment Journal. She brings a well-rounded and grounded approach to communicating with the angelic realm. Live an empowered, healthy, energized life through developing and trusting in your own natural intuitive abilities. Learn more about Cindy Smith AEP™ ATP® at *www.cindysmithaep.com*

Spiritual Authors Circle

This co-created community of spiritual writers, authors, lightworkers and messengers is created to provide a platform for our books, services and contributions to spread our message of Unity Consciousness. You can learn all about our conscious network of a million lightworkers and messengers that will be sharing their spiritual products and services on this site, along with bonuses and links to their websites. Please visit *www.spiritualauthorscircle.com*.

ABOUT THE AUTHOR

KAREN MCGREGOR, M.Ed., is an international speaker and author with a passionate commitment to the Divine Feminine. Karen offers Divine Feminine lectures, experiential seminars, women's circles and conferences. Through her company, DivineYou.ca, Karen hosts bestselling spiritual authors, on-line courses and teleseminars. She also facilitates two spiritual writing groups and an on-line writing community.

A former business workshop facilitator and speaker, Karen wrote and published her first book four years ago, while interviewing entrepreneurs about their success practices. *Sculpting the Business Body: Strategies and Stories from Top Entrepreneurs,* illustrates the depth of insight and intuition of some of Canada's leading business owners. Her community honored her dedication to women's business associations and women entrepreneurs with a nomination for the 2007 Women of Excellence Awards in Langley, British Columbia, Canada.

While preparing to write *The Madonna Code: Mysteries of the Divine Feminine Unveiled,* Karen created *Your Path to Miracles* CD and DVD. They serve as a wise and practical guide to heightening consciousness at home, in your community and beyond through the power of radical love.

She lives with her two sons in a green oasis, surrounded by the vibrant Lower Mainland of Vancouver, British Columbia, Canada.

LaVergne, TN USA
16 November 2010
205008LV00004B/1/P